W9-BKX-512

As Bill Nix points out in *Transforming Your Workplace for Christ,* the Golden Rule should not be left at the door when returning to work on Monday morning. Through their Christian faith, the founding families of Amway believe each individual is unique as created by God and have treated employees accordingly as all being essential members of a team. Such values transform a workplace by encouraging people to succeed to the fullest extent of their potential.

Dick DeVos, President,
Amway Corporation

I like Bill Nix and I like this book! Bill is really hitting the nail on the head and driving it in with wisdom and class. I need this outlook on my business career and really believe every Christian professional needs it too!

Joe T. White, President,
Kanakuk-Kanakomo Kamps

Bill Nix's book tackles one of the most important areas of Christian life imaginable. There is nothing more crucial for Christians to learn than integrating Christ into their work, and Bill has produced an outstanding tool. The interweaving of principle and practical example make it extremely useful!

Frank M. Barker Jr., Pastor,
Briarwood Presbyterian Church,
Birmingham, Alabama

Bill Nix has written the kind of book that every pastor wants in the hands of his laity. This pertinent volume is biblical, practical, and readable. My prayer is that it will have wide distribution.

Adrian Rogers, Pastor,
Bellevue Baptist Church,
Cordova, Tennessee

Transforming Your Workplace for Christ

Transforming Your Workplace for Christ

WILLIAM NIX

FOREWORD BY JOHN TRENT

BROADMAN
&HOLMAN
PUBLISHERS

Nashville, Tennessee

© 1997 by William H. Nix
All rights reserved
Printed in the United States of America

Published by Broadman & Holman Publishers, Nashville, Tennessee
Acquisitions & Development Editor: John Landers
Interior Design: Desktop Miracles, Addison, Texas

4262-90
0-8054-6290-2

Dewey Decimal Classification: 248.5
Subject Heading: CHRISTIAN LIFE / EVANGELISTIC WORK
Library of Congress Card Catalog Number: 96-51759

Unless otherwise noted, Scripture quotations are from the Holy Bible, New International Version, copyright © 1973, 1978, 1984 by International Bible Society. Passages marked NASB are from the New American Standard Bible, © the Lockman Foundation, 1960, 1962, 1963, 1968, 1971, 1972, 1973, 1975, 1977, used by permission; KJV, the King James Version.

Library of Congress Cataloging-in-Publication Data
Nix, William H., 1959–
    Transforming your workplace for Christ / William H. Nix.
        p.   cm.
    ISBN 0-8054-6290-2 (pbk.)
    1. Witness bearing (Christianity).   2. Business—Religious aspects—
Christianity.   3. Business ethics.   4. Christian ethics—Baptist authors.
5. Nix, William H., 1959– . I. Title.
BV4520.N55   1997
248'.5—dc21

96-51759
CIP

97 98 99 00 01   5 4 3 2 1

To my wife, Teri, whose prayer, wisdom, and integrity have helped keep me on the path with God. Thank you for giving me the freedom to transform my workplace for Christ. I thank God that He picked you to work with me to transform our home for Christ.

Contents

Foreword

I remember the first time I mentioned the tremendous work Bill Nix was doing at helping win his company for Christ. It was at a seminar where I was sharing about building godly relationships. In talking about building godly character in an increasingly godless world, I mentioned, "And let's not forget about the workplace. I have a good friend named Bill Nix who has an entire program on how not only to teach Christian values in the workplace, but how to win his company for Christ." I was shocked to discover what happened at the break.

Forget everything I'd said up to that point in the seminar. I was swamped by men and women who came up to me and asked, "Tell me more about that Bill Nix guy and what he's doing in the workplace. How can I get hold of him? Does he have anything in print?"

That's when I knew that Bill had hit a raw nerve, uncovering a piercing need in the Christian community. We have shelves of books and teachers that tell us how to live for Christ. But I can't think of another book like this one that can specifically show you how to live out your faith in your workplace.

You may be the boss or the third assistant to the fourth assistant. But whether you've got twenty years under your belt or are only beginning your career, you've found the right resource to help make Christ more a part of your eight-to-five, and more known to others around you. From understanding the key role Christian values play in advancing His kingdom (and your career), to gaining a five-step plan to capture your company for Christ, it's all here. And it's written by someone who's been there, done that, and got the T-shirt that says, "I made a difference for Jesus Christ in the lives of those I worked with."

As a marriage and family counselor, I've seen the inner struggle many men and women battle. It's almost like they're living in two worlds. One world is the dog-eat-dog workplace where being a Christian is the same as being "politically incorrect" and Christ is a name flippantly taken in vain. The other world is when they drive out of the parking lot and flip on Christian radio as they drive home.

Wouldn't it be great to see those two worlds become one?

I'm convinced the answer isn't for you to ditch your workplace and join a monastery. It's to stay where you are and begin to capture your workplace—any workplace—for Christ. Imagine getting up in the morning not dreading but dedicated to going to work for a purpose—His purpose for you in your workplace! You may never change the entire corporate culture where you work, but you can change lives—your own and many others as well. And you've got a wonderful brother and his helpful book to help you begin the change process.

I know Bill Nix. I've met his wife and children, and talked with those who have worked with him in the trenches of the work-a-day world. I whole-heartedly support what he's doing right now through his Faith at Work ministry and what he's written in this book. May his insights into living for Christ in the place most of us spend most of our time bless encourage, and inspire you. And may you indeed, capture your workplace for Christ.

John Trent, Ph.D.
Author/Speaker
President, Encouraging Words

Acknowledgments

God used Promise Keepers to communicate the vision to me for this project. Thank you, Coach Bill McCartney, Randy Phillips, and the crew at PK for following God's leadership. Thank you, Tank Tankersley, Mark and Chris Anderson, Eddie and Evelyn Parker, Bruce and Gini Hose, and Paul and Barb Till for your encouraging words every time we are together. If there is a modern day Barnabas, it has to be my pastor, Jay Wolf. Thanks for being there at just the right times. Steve and Elizabeth Barrington read every word of this book and loved me enough to tell me what they liked and what they did not like. Thank you for investing a lot of time to help me hone the message. Broadman & Holman's John Landers and Bucky Rosenbaum: Thank you for exercising your patience and expertise.

My family is one of God's great blessings in my life. My father, Earl Nix, is with the Lord. He was a person intent on transforming his workplace and his world for Christ. My mother, Hazel Nix, is a daily source of encouragement to me. Likewise, Teri's parents, Jerry and Becky Washington, have supported us unconditionally. Chip and Michelle Nix (my brother and sister-in-law) and Randy and Luanne Hamilton (my brother-in-law and sister) always supported me in prayer. I can't imagine having a greater family.

I have saved John Trent to the end because he was there in the beginning. It was John Trent who first saw the work I was doing in a mortgage company and said, "Others would benefit from your experience." Thank you for the initial instruction, constant encouragement, and eternal friendship.

Introduction

In July 1993 I sat with fifty thousand men listening to James Dobson speak to the gathering of Promise Keepers in Boulder. "When you come to the end of your life," Dobson said, "the only thing that will matter will be who you loved, who loved you, and what you did in service for your Creator." That one statement made my long trek to Boulder worthwhile. Dobson's words found a permanent spot in my soul. My life goals were clarified.

I asked myself, *Does my life's priority today match those Dobson said will matter at the end of my life?* Answering that question naturally led me to ask, *Am I working today in a way that will be pleasing at the end of my life? Does my work today honor God?*

I had been working in the banking industry for sixteen years— for ten years as an investment banker and six years as chief operating officer of a mortgage company. I was honest. I worked hard. That had to be pleasing to God. Yet I asked myself, *Is there more to honoring God through my work than simply being honest and working hard?*

The answer surprised and excited me. I knew that God created our work for a purpose and placed us in that work to honor Him. Jesus met people in the course of their work more often than anywhere else. He called His disciples while they were at work. He met the woman at the well in the course of her labor. Jesus taught using workplace illustrations such as the wise and foolish builders (Matt. 7:24–27), the workers in the vineyard (Matt. 20:1–16), the shrewd manager (Luke 16:1–8), and the rich fool (Luke 12:16–21).

Jesus was known as a carpenter. He had developed a skill, and He must have employed that skill. Interestingly, though, there is little mention of His trade. Perhaps that is because Christ did not distinguish His practical work as a carpenter from His ministry. Maybe working as a carpenter opened the door for His work as a minister.

Does your work open doors for your ministry? It should. I heard Stephen Chalk, a minister in England, tell the story of his friend who was a mortgage banker. The friend told Chalk that he sensed a call to join the ranks of the clergy. Chalk responded, "You would make a mediocre clergyman. But you are an awesome mortgage banker. Be a minister where you are. Penetrate the mortgage banking world for Christ."

Bankers, electricians, lawyers, doctors, policemen, production line workers, nurses, and cab drivers—listen! God gave you work to honor Him. God gave you work to open the door for ministry in His name. You may be one of the legions who are unfulfilled by their work. Maybe you are looking for that fulfillment. Ask yourself, *Is my work part of my ministry?* Perhaps you have had a mountaintop experience such as Promise Keepers. You may be sensing a call to join the ranks of the clergy. Before you enroll in seminary and move your family to a far off place, answer these questions: Am I honoring God with my work? Am I using my work to open doors of ministry right where I am?

Your life can be marked by ministry. Be intentional about trying to transform your workplace for Christ. This book challenges you with an appropriate, effective, and scriptural way to bring Christ to your workplace. When you honor God by capturing your workplace for Christ, three things will happen:

❖ You will experience fulfillment you have never before known.
❖ Your coworkers will be drawn to you.
❖ Your relationship with God will grow to an exciting new level.

You can help transform your company for Christ by living out the ten character qualities and taking the five steps described in this book.

Ten Christian Values
Every Workplace
Needs

1

Love
The Unexpected Action

The Kathy Montgomery Story

Kathy Montgomery's day started like any other day. She paused to look over the hills of her family's farm, scrolling the day's activities through her mind. As a wife, mother of three, and kindergarten teacher, she had a busy day ahead of her, including a routine medical check-up in the afternoon.

Though she had a tough day at school, her characteristic smile and laugh greeted the physician and nurses. Kathy patiently made her way through the maze of tests, x-rays, and needle pricks to the exam room. Dangling her feet from the examination table, she reflected on the day. Soon her physician entered to begin his review of Kathy's condition. Everything looked fine; that is, until he performed a breast exam.

Suddenly Kathy's otherwise ordinary day took a detour. She sensed from the pained expression on the doctor's face that he detected a big problem. For the first time in her forty-seven years, Kathy heard her doctor mention the possibility of cancer.

Her physician ordered tests, and the diagnosis was confirmed: breast cancer had invaded her body. The outlook was not encouraging. On a scale of one to four, Kathy's cancer was classified 3B—one notch below the worst possible. To complicate matters, it had spread to her lymph nodes. She needed a mastectomy, followed by chemotherapy, radiation, and perhaps a bone marrow transplant.

A thousand thoughts flooded Kathy's mind. Trust in the God who had so richly blessed her life undergirded her concern for her three daughters and her husband, John. But what about her other children—her kindergarten students? How would her illness and upcoming treatment impact her ability to teach? How would her employers react? Would she need to resign and make way for another teacher? If not, what would she do if she felt too sick to teach one day? What if a substitute could not be found? Fear swept over her.

Two Options

Brian Willett and Darlene Mullen struggled to run a Christian school. Every day they wrestled with state and federal regulations and worked diligently to pay the bills. Mr. Willett was headmaster of Trinity Presbyterian School, and Dr. Mullen was responsible for Trinity's elementary school, which included the kindergarten where Kathy Montgomery taught.

Kathy met with Willett and Mullen to tell them of her illness. The trio had worked together for years, and their feelings for each other ran deep.

Willett and Mullen immediately thought of two options. But which was better? Option 1 was to follow standard operating procedures: A sick teacher calls a substitute; if he or she cannot locate a substitute, Dr. Mullen will assist.

Then there was option 2: Dr. Mullen could convince Kathy that it was in her best interest and the children's best interest for her to take an extended leave of absence without pay.

Both options seemed reasonable. After all, the school had to go forward. Wasn't the school's efficient and profitable operation more important than any individual employee? And the burden on Kathy to call in sick was not too much to ask, right? Well, it looked OK on paper, but neither option satisfied Willett's and Mullen's desire to show Kathy how much they and the school valued and loved her.

Love's Third Option

Willett and Mullen discovered option 3: The school had a financial reserve that had resulted from years of prudent management.

Trinity could use those funds to hire another teacher to assist Kathy every day and to carry the load on days Kathy was too ill to be there.

This is what they decided to do. Not only were the critical needs met, but Trinity's expression of love toward Kathy also honored our Lord, who said, "By this all men will know that you are My disciples, if you have love for one another" (John 13:35, NASB).

How would you have handled this situation? Conventional wisdom in the workplace today suggests the individual is not as important as the aggregate group of coworkers. No one would have blamed you if you had chosen option 1. Would you have seized this salty opportunity to honor God by expressing love toward another?

Maybe you are not the headmaster of a school or the senior executive of your workplace. Maybe you are one of the millions who work under the authority of others. If so, you probably are not forced to make decisions like the one made by Willett and Mullen. Yet there are many opportunities for you to express God's love each day in your workplace. In fact, each of us must look for ways to share God's love, regardless of where our names appear on the organizational chart.

Judy's Unexpected Action

I stepped into an elevator once with Judy Fuhrer, a customer service representative of a mid–sized firm. She was holding a beautiful green plant wrapped nicely in a white bow. I was somewhat curious, so I asked Judy what occasion prompted the plant. Her birthday or anniversary seemed logical to me. But once again, the response was unexpected. Judy's coworker, Casey Fults, was mourning the loss of her father–in–law and was due back to work the next day. Judy and the other members of the customer service department simply wanted Casey to know they cared. Simple? Sure. But what a powerful expression of love!

Do you see yourself in this example of the unexpected action? Everybody in an organization can express Christlike love the way this customer service clan demonstrated. You can express God's love at your place of employment.

Jimmy Meets Kay: Is This Love?

Jimmy and his wife had been married twenty years, but Jimmy thought she was no longer capable of meeting his needs. Their conversations fell flat. Jimmy's interests now differed greatly from those things that interested her. He woke up one morning and realized that he had outgrown his wife—or so he thought.

Jimmy managed thirty bank employees, and Kay was his secretary. Like her boss, Kay had begun to feel distanced from her husband. In fact, her husband irritated Kay on a regular basis. Work became an oasis for Kay, a retreat where she went for consolation about her frustrating life.

Jimmy and Kay began discussing their problems and consoling each other. Each agreed that the other had a horrible home and a malicious mate. Soon all that was needed to consummate the betrayal was an opportunity.

A conference in Boston was the opportunity Jimmy and Kay needed. Before long their tryst was a well–known "secret" around the office. Many people knew about it, yet nobody confronted Jimmy or Kay. No one asked the hard questions about the effect their self-centered, pleasure-seeking joy ride was having at home. Some even played along with the deception.

Coworkers began considering Jimmy and Kay a couple. Some admired their "love" for each other. A few even provided cover by having lunch with them so they would not appear to be a couple. Others spoke despairingly about the two unsuspecting spouses. After a while the inevitable divorces were complete, making way for Jimmy and Kay to come out into the open.

The case of Jimmy and Kay is no isolated affair. Workplaces everywhere are abuzz about these "love" liaisons. But is this really love?

The Love Test

Are you concerned about something going on in your workplace? Perhaps it is clear to discern, like the case of Jimmy and Kay. Perhaps it is not so clear, and you wonder how to respond. If so, two questions can help you decide whether actions or relationships in your workplace demonstrate genuine Christlike love.

Question 1: Is my action or relationship consistent with God's Word? Jesus told Philip, "If you love me, you will obey what I command" (John 14:15). Something may feel good, something may be convenient, but that is not a valid test. True love must obey Christ's commands. Jimmy and Kay satisfied what they thought were their own needs, but they violated Christ's commands. How about you? Are you flirting with a coworker? Are you using a coworker to make yourself look good in the eyes of your supervisor? Perhaps you just crushed the spirit of a colleague in your race up the career ladder. Are your actions consistent with the commands of Scripture? Would Christ be proud of your relationships?

Question 2: Can I tell everybody about this action or relationship? In the Sermon on the Mount, Jesus instructed His disciples, "Let your light shine before men, that they may see your good deeds and praise your Father in heaven" (Matt. 5:16). Illicit relationships and mean-spirited actions are almost always concealed. The wrongdoer acts in secret. But Jesus tells us to obey His commands so that our actions and our relationships will stand up for the whole unbelieving world to see. Does your life on the job reflect the love of Christ?

You probably remember Jesus' story of the good Samaritan. (If not, you can read it in Luke 10:30–37.) Do your actions on the job resemble those of the robber? Or are you more like the priest and Levite who crossed the road and continued on their way. Perhaps you are most like the Samaritan who encountered the victim and "took pity on him." If so, then your coworkers are blessed, just as Kathy Montgomery and her family were blessed. If you have followed Christ's command to love, your coworkers have been comforted as Casey Fults was comforted. If you are a modern-day good Samaritan, then you have shown your coworkers the Christlike look of love.

The Look of His Love

Most of us dread Monday morning. I often hear comments like "It has been Monday morning all day." Upon asking a coworker how they feel on this first day back to work, I typically hear, "It is Monday morning, isn't it?"

Why do we so often drag ourselves into Monday? Perhaps it is because the oasis of a weekend full of family, recreation, and generally fun activities comes to an abrupt halt when the alarm clock sounds off on Monday morning. Certainly our reluctance to break with these coveted times is understandable. But could there be an explanation that goes deeper—to the very heart of who we are as Christians? Could there be a dark side to this question that many of us have not faced?

Sunday morning you leaped out of bed preparing for worship and fellowship with other believers. You put on your best attire and made your way to church. You worshiped, prayed, and maybe you even taught a Sunday school class. Great! But now on Monday things are different. Although you wear the same dress or suit that you wore to church the previous day, your countenance has changed. You are going to work, not to church. Life is different at work, right? You can't act like you do at church because the world of work demands that you behave a certain way to get ahead, right?

If you have made these statements, then you have answered the Monday morning mystery. I believe part of the reason we dread Monday morning is that we have accepted the above statements as true. We lead a double life! We actually believe that our work lives are separate from our life of following Christ. We have bought into the lie that says to succeed you must behave in ways that dishonor God.

On the heels of a day of worshiping the one true God and marveling in His majesty we awaken to the reality of our double life. There is a word for this unpleasant circumstance—sin. If you are caught in this trap, then major alarms should be sounding at this moment. Please hear these words from my heart. We Christians can seek God's forgiveness and find redemption for our disobedience. I encourage you to ask God for forgiveness right now! Then seek to unify your life into one that pursues God consistently, regardless of the day of the week and regardless of your venue.

Christians must personify Christ daily for the world of lost souls who need to find Christ. If they ever see the gospel in action, they will have to see it in us. Those lost souls show up for work on Monday mornings just like we do. And we must accept the fact that they watch their Christian counterparts. Non-believers are evidence seekers, mining our lives to see if we reveal the pure gold of God or the fool's gold of the world.

God must shed a tear when one of His own causes a non-believer to say, "Did you see how Joe treated me? And he says he is a Christian!" Examine your actions while at work. Is your life at work consistent with God's command to love one another? Does your life bear the look of His love? If so, the following six characteristics will be evident in your actions.

Kindness

During your drive into work on any maddening Monday you probably begin to roll over in your mind the tasks that are staring you in the face. You left a project hanging over the weekend that you must finish. You need to solve a problem caused by a coworker's mistake. You must meet with another coworker who is angry. Your overbearing boss expects a report just as soon as you arrive. Although you feel a little overwhelmed, you determine to focus on the tasks ahead. You plan to tackle the mountain of work the way your boss believes it should be done—even though you may bruise a coworker's spirit or be a little rude at times.

But what does the "Big Boss" say? Our God and Creator says of Himself, "I am the LORD, who exercises kindness" (Jer. 9:24). Through His prophet, God spoke these words to a disobedient people.

How much more then should you show kindness to those people in the next office. You know them; they are the evidence seekers. Kindness is so important in our daily walk that the apostle Paul included this naturally Christlike action in the short list of the fruits of the Spirit found in Galatians 5:22–23. The world is hungry for Christlike kindness. The people at your place of employment are hungry for Christlike kindness.

During the transition from King Solomon's leadership to the leadership of his son Rehoboam, the people of Israel requested that Rehoboam treat them fairly. For too long the people had been subjected to Solomon's harsh rule. Rehoboam consulted his elders who advised, "If you will be kind to these people and please them and give them a favorable answer, they will always be your servants" (2 Chron. 10:7). Rehoboam rejected the elders' advice, and the people of Israel rebelled against his rule.

The Israelites wanted to be treated kindly. Possibly the most visible evidence of Christ's love is the kindness you show to others. Regardless of your position at work, you can reveal Christ to a hurting work force by showing kindness to your coworkers.

Janet arrived for work to find a pink slip on her desk. She was being laid off. Her only task was to gather up her personal items and head home. Robin, her coworker, took her break early so she could help Janet pack her things. Though Robin knew she could be the next one laid off, she stepped beyond the anxiety of her own circumstance to reveal a kindness that could only come from Christ.

"He who is kind to the poor lends to the LORD, and he will reward him for what he has done" (Prov. 19:17). The poor in spirit, the poor in worldly wealth, the poor in confidence, the poor at work all need our kindness because they all need our Savior. This proverb tells us that Robin's kind of kindness is noticed by the Lord, and He blesses us in response.

Patience

Barbara moved to our city when her husband's company transferred him. She had excellent experience in a job similar to an opening we were trying to fill. Barbara was very impressive, and we hired her rather quickly.

A year passed. We had reengineered our company, and this cast Barbara in a slightly different role. Responsibilities were shifted around, but almost everyone was adapting to new procedures. While Barbara and her family were vacationing, a question arose regarding an area for which she was responsible. Barbara's supervisor rummaged through her desk trying to find the papers necessary to answer the question. Instead, the supervisor found a mound of work that had not been completed. Some of the work dated back six months.

Barbara's supervisor met with me and said, "We have a termination set up for Monday." The supervisor explained how Barbara had hoarded a pile of work, and she wanted to take care of the situation by terminating Barbara's employment. A review of Barbara's personnel file showed no problems in the past.

I heard the arguments in favor of letting Barbara go, but I was not convinced this ultimate employment action was necessary or fair, much less honoring to our Lord. That's right! I believe we must filter all business decisions through the Word of God. His Word is applicable even in personnel-related matters. In fact, His Word is applicable *especially* in personnel-related matters.

I explained to the supervisor that, in my opinion, we had hired Barbara with too high an expectation and that the misperception of her abilities was our fault, not Barbara's. Knowing that Barbara was not malicious in her sloppy work, I asked the supervisor to consider how she would want to be treated if she were in Barbara's place. Then I asked her to call me the next morning to discuss an appropriate response to Barbara's work performance.

A biblical response awaited me the next morning. These words of the apostle Paul sum up the supervisor's response: "Warn those who are idle, encourage the timid, help the weak, be patient with everyone" (1 Thess. 5:14). Barbara was warned to improve her work. She was given training in certain areas to shore up her weak spots. Later she transferred to another area of the company, and now she is doing a great job. Patience saved the day and made a Christ-honoring difference in Barbara's life.

Paul, in 1 Timothy, speaks of Christ's "unlimited patience" (v. 16) in bringing about the eternal change in his life. At times it seems that we too must exhibit unlimited patience in a world that desires to have it all today. In many workplaces Barbara would have been released on the spot. If someone in the ranks cannot measure up, then cut them loose. The growth of a business or institution and, yes, even a church has become more important than the very souls of those doing the building.

Certainly I believe in efficient and timely management, but my greatest sense of urgency is for the lost souls of those I work with. James writes, "Be patient, then, brothers, until the Lord's coming. See how the farmer waits for the land to yield its valuable crop and how patient he is for the fall and spring rains. You too, be patient and stand firm, because the Lord's coming is near" (James 5:7–8).

You may be frustrated with a coworker or baffled by your boss. Your business may not be developing at the pace you had planned. You may be desiring new work. Maybe your coworkers or supervisors misunderstand you. Be patient! "Be still before the LORD and wait patiently for him; do not fret when men succeed in their ways, when they carry out their wicked schemes. . . . Those who hope in the LORD will inherit the land" (Ps. 37:7, 9). Take on His unlimited patience and stand firm in your faith, and through your present difficulty Christ will conform you to His image; in the process, He will reveal Himself to those with whom you work.

All-encompassing Love

Look around your workplace. If it is like most, you see persons of every color representing a microcosm of the economic spectrum. Young and old, male and female, believers and non-believers. You see a diverse group of people with a wide variety of needs, experiences, and opinions.

Now look again at your coworkers. This time look deep into their eyes and try to discern their needs. The mountain of needs may scare you. The needs may repulse you. As you ponder the souls of these needful people, do you find their yearnings uninteresting? Are you unwilling to attempt to meet these needs?

We serve a God of unlimited capacity to meet needs, a God who offers His love unconditionally. Do you show God's love unconditionally? Much has been written about demonstrating unconditional love within our families. This uncommon, limitless love is desperately needed at home. But I believe God also expects us to pack our briefcases and lunchboxes with His all-encompassing love and take it with us to work.

Ron Stallworth, a mountain of a man with a true heart for God, was a coworker of mine. During one of our Wednesday Bible study meetings, we discussed Christ's words: "For my Father's will is that everyone who looks to the Son and believes in him shall have eternal life" (John 6:40). Ron helped me reflect on my efforts to transform my workplace for Christ. As an African American, Ron's presence forced me to consider my efforts to reach out to my African American coworkers. Our group discussed ways to cross

racial lines on behalf of our Lord at work and elsewhere. I personally took the challenge articulated by Coach Bill McCartney, founder
of Promise Keepers. Looking Ron in the eye, I apologized for both
the sin of my forefathers and my own sin. I then asked Ron if we
could go forward unified in our witness.

People in your workplace need Christ's message of unconditional and unlimited love. Maybe their need stems from past racial
prejudices. Maybe you work with someone who is economically dis-
advantaged. Maybe the person one desk over is simply not attractive.
Whatever their need, you have the answer in Christ's unconditional
love.

What would your attitude be toward Jimmy and Kay if they
worked with you? If they repented, how would you treat them? And
exactly how would you handle their situation? Would you confront
them in a loving way? Or would you only talk behind their backs?

Christ offers guidance for such a situation. John 8:1–11 records
the story of a woman caught in an adulterous relationship. The
teachers of the law asked Jesus what they should do with her as they
began to gather up stones. Jesus simply knelt down and began doodling in the dirt. Some have suggested that Jesus was writing the
names of those in the crowd along with their sins. Whatever He was
writing caught the attention of the would-be executioners. They
stopped their planned stoning so they could hear Jesus speak. The
woman's sin was exposed, but she was protected.

All-encompassing, Christlike love protects the sinner while
attacking the sin. Jimmy and Kay were certainly discussed during
breaks and lunch hours. Were you there? Did you participate in the
gossip? Did you find it more compelling to attack the sinners and
forget about the sin? If Christ were in your place of employment, I
believe He would be doodling in the dirt, and so should we.

Working with those who differ from us can be challenging.
Looking beyond our differences to see the God-given talent in each
individual while demonstrating unconditional love is necessary to
effectively represent Christ. Protecting others from ridicule and hurt
is a Christlike action others will respect. If you incorporate these elements of Christlike love into your life, your effectiveness as a witness
for Him will skyrocket!

Trust

Our work is very important to each one of us, but we sometimes forget that it is also important to God. We frequently strike out on our own at work, leaving God at home. Human nature causes us to believe the old saying: "If it is to be, it is up to me." Why don't we trust God with this area of our lives?

Our chronic lack of trust in our Creator concerning this vital area of our lives causes us to dishonor Christ by our actions. When we only trust in our own ability to get a promotion, then we often step on someone else in the process. When our trust does not extend beyond the work of our own hands, then we often jab our coworkers.

Jane Folk, an executive with General Electric Mortgage Corporation, witnessed an uncommon demonstration of Christlike trust. A management-level job opened up at her office. This plum position was open for employees to apply and a number of her coworkers submitted their résumés. One of Jane's coworkers was unsure how he should write his résumé, but a colleague helped him rewrite it so that it emphasized his experience most closely related to the duties of the open position. Now the surprise: the résumé coach was also applying for the job!

What a powerful example of trust in God! By his actions this résumé writer told his coworkers that his trust was in God. It really did not matter that he helped his associate apply because God is in control, and we can trust God to bring about His good purpose in our lives (Rom. 8:28). The man trusted his associate because he first trusted God.

You may not be competing for a promotion right now, but perhaps your trust is in question. Think about your colleagues. Is someone's ability or motivation in question? Christlike love compels you to trust them and to show this trust by believing in the best possible outcome.

Think of Barbara's case. Her supervisor was ready to fire her and even suggested that Barbara may have been dishonest with our company. I made this manager focus on the best possible reason for Barbara's weakness at work. The supervisor was told to trust Barbara.

Christlike love causes us to trust our colleagues. Christlike love compels us to confidently believe the best in others. Trusting others at work is possible if you are trusting God with your life.

Hope

I hired a new manager for an office in the western United States. Our expectations of this man were quite high, but his office's production did not meet our expectations. We were disappointed. It was clear I needed to make a trip to his office and discuss the situation. Arrangements were made that best fit his schedule. A coworker asked me why I was making the trip on that day. I responded, "Because that day was best for his schedule." The questioner was shocked and asked, "Why are you working around his schedule? He needs to work around yours! Anyway, he is probably not going to make it."

My caustic coworker had lost hope in our man in the West. I had not. I believed it was my responsibility to have unlimited hope in this man and to turn that hope into action. I chose to fit into his schedule so he could maximize his time producing business for our company. I was hopeful that the producer would turn his performance around.

We must show this kind of hope to a lost world at work because Christ demonstrated His kind of hope with us. Consider Peter's plight. Peter denied Christ not once, not twice, but three times (Luke 22:54–62). How did Jesus respond? He did not tell Peter to come back when His schedule was lighter. Christ did not tell Peter he would not make it. No, Christ demonstrated His unique hope by embracing Peter and giving him another chance.

We serve the God of second chances because we serve the God of hope. As His servants, we must demonstrate a hope for our colleagues that can only come from God.

Endurance

Expressing God's love in the workplace is hard. Sometimes we are labeled "too soft" for the demands and challenges.

Once a coworker told me my image among my peers and those in positions above mine had suffered because I did not appear tough enough. He suggested I demonstrate a "tougher" persona or advancement would be limited for me. I was dumbfounded, but I managed to ask him two questions:

❖ What was it about me that gave him the impression that I was not tough enough?
❖ Just how tough did I have to be to succeed?

He replied, "You go longer with people than we do," and "Your personality is so constant!" He continued, "If you want to ascend to a higher chair, you need to learn to jerk some chains every now and then."

The easy response would have been to agree and change my style to conform with the others around me. Yet at that moment I was reminded that transforming my workplace for Christ would not be easy. Ridicule was a cross I would have to bear. Promotions might not come my way if I chose to stay the Christlike course. Conform to our worldly way of building this business or get prepared to be trampled was the inherent message I received that day.

Honestly, I never considered abandoning the loveship of Christ. Endurance was the key for me that day; endurance remains the key for me today. It is the element of love that tests our commitment to Christ.

Noah is a good example of endurance. God told him to build an ark of specific dimensions and materials. Noah followed His orders. Can you imagine what the neighbors said? Can't you picture the expression on the faces of those who worked around Noah? Noah was ridiculed, but he trusted God and endured. He stayed on the godly course, and today we have a rainbow to prove it!

God's love never fails, and it never ends. Christlike love is kind, patient, all-encompassing, trusting, hopeful, and endures forever. The following activities can help you develop these Christlike qualities:

❖ List these Christlike traits of love down the left side of a sheet of paper. Space the words at least two inches apart. In the blank spaces, write specific ways you can model these traits at your place of employment.

❖ From the list of action points, make a schedule of times you can demonstrate the love of Christ.

Love's Result

All Christians should desire to serve and please God, but few Christians step out in faith and move counter to our culture. This is especially true in our work lives. Yet my experience has taught me that the real joy of our walk with Christ comes when we press against the edge of our comfort zone.

New and Improved Meaning

If you represent Christ boldly at your place of employment, God will bless you by giving your work new meaning. Brian Willet and Darlene Mullen received such a blessing. These two educators had no idea how God would use their handling of Kathy Montgomery's tragic illness. They had no idea that Kathy would spend the last eight weeks of school confined to a bone marrow transplant unit. They did not see up-front how hiring Kay Goggans as Kathy's coteacher would benefit the children and make a powerful statement of Christlike love to the adults in the community. They simply were trying to help Kathy and show her the uncommon love of Christ.

Today, Willett and Mullen have a renewed joy about their work. They see clearly how God takes a difficult work issue and uses it for His glory. Trinity School will be better than ever. The Christ-honoring leadership of Willett and Mullen has given God a platform to reveal Himself. Motivated and energized by God's rich blessing on their lives, Willett and Mullen have found new and improved meaning in their work.

Fulfill the Great Commission

Thousands of people in our community and beyond have been touched by Kathy's circumstance. A big part of the story being told is how Kathy's employers glorified God in their workplace. Many have been challenged by Trinity's example. Many have been blessed by such a bold witness.

My family is among the blessed. Our son Will was a student in Kathy's class the year she was diagnosed with cancer. She went home to be with the Lord the evening of June 9, 1995. The morning of June 10, 1995, Will accepted Christ as his Savior. That morning I met with Will and our oldest daughter, Lauren, in our den. Lauren was nine at the time and had been a believer for two years. Will had been seeking the Lord. He had been in Kathy's class for about six months and understood the reason Kay Goggans was helping with the class. Will knew that Mr. Willett and Dr. Mullen hired her because they loved God, Mrs. Montgomery, and him. When he understood the reality of Kathy's death and the Christlike witness of the Trinity leadership, Will surrendered his life to Christ. His response was appropriate and a testimony to the love of God. Only God sees the full effect of our bold actions for Him. Willett and Mullen certainly did not foresee Will's entering the family of faith as a result of their actions, but God used their work to bring about an eternal change in the life of my son. Praise God!

Conformity to Christ

Your bold witness at work will bear fruit. God honors actions of Christlike love. You may not know what God will do, but you can be confident He is at work. Maybe His work is with you, or maybe He is working through you to reach your coworkers.

Barbara was spared termination of her employment. After the initial meeting when Barbara was confronted about her work, the supervisor came to my office bearing a peaceful countenance. "The meeting went well," he said. "Barbara had such a peace about her and such a wonderful spirit! I was just amazed."

Conformity. Not to the ways of the world but to Christ. The supervisor noticed something radically different about Barbara. Barbara used this difficulty in her life to grow more in the likeness of Christ.

Paul wrote, "I do not understand what I do. For what I want to do I do not do, but what I hate I do" (Rom. 7:15). Indeed, we live in a

confused world. It desperately needs the love of Christ, yet it seems to reject His free offer of love at every turn. Workplaces are composed of people who need the love of Christ, but many working cultures behave in ways that dishonor Him. To get ahead in the world's eye you often must selfishly step ahead of someone else— sometimes even step on top of another person. This is expected behavior. Yet Christians often are called to do the unexpected. When a follower of Jesus Christ steps forward to transform his or her workplace for Christ, others notice.

Love—this unexpected action—is the first step toward transforming your workplace for Christ.

2

Encouragement
The Eternal Intervention

Bill and Millie Morgan did what they knew had to be done. They did not stop to think about what lay ahead. They did not pause to reflect on all the possible ramifications of their actions. The thought never occurred to them that their endeavor might be difficult and that their efforts might accomplish little if any positive results.

This encouraging couple saw a need—a need that was time sensitive, a need that would not wait while they weighed the pro's and con's of getting involved. Hesitation would have been dangerous. Procrastination would have been catastrophic. Rationalizing that someone else could meet this need would have been easy, but it might have been a death sentence for Ken Sawyer.

You Can't Stay the Same and Go with God

By March 1983 Ken Sawyer had been employed by Bill Morgan for five years. Bill and Millie frequently planned social outings for the employees in Bill's office. The Morgans and Ken became good friends. Millie tried her hand at matchmaking a few times, and Bill periodically invited Ken to attend their church. Though Ken dated a few of Millie's finds and attended their church on occasion, there seemed to be no positive spiritual result from their efforts.

When the phone rang late one night, the Morgans received the message that Ken had been involved in a serious traffic accident. Without hesitation or discussion, Bill and Millie dressed and rushed to the hospital. Speculation was high that Ken had been drinking.

The emergency room was teeming with activity that night. Nurses and doctors worked at a frantic pace. An attendant ushered the Morgans to a cubicle strutting a cotton cloth wall. The attendant pulled the divider back to reveal the victim of a horrific collision between a train and a car. Ken was so badly broken that some of his friends did not recognize him. The left side of his face was crushed, and five ribs were snapped.

Millie and Bill's worst fear was confirmed: Ken had been so drunk that he never saw the train. Now he was a mess. With blood from head to toe, his face grossly disfigured, Ken's painful moan touched the Morgans that night.

Many people, especially employers, might have inquired about Ken's condition and then left for a comfortable night of sleep. Not Bill and Millie Morgan. They did not see a bloody bag of bones lying on the hospital bed; they saw a man in need, a man with an unlimited future in Christ. The Morgans, full of faith, saw an opportunity to intervene in Ken's life, ever hopeful that an eternal change would occur.

Millie felt compelled to stay with Ken that night. She held his hand and patted his forehead with a cool cloth, responding to his moans with comforting words.

Ken eventually returned to work. Bill greeted him warmly and invited him into his office. In a loving and kind manner, Bill discussed Ken's obvious drinking problem and his need for help. Incredibly, Ken dismissed Bill's concern, describing the wreck as a freak occurrence that would not happen again. Still, Bill and Millie never gave up on Ken.

Ken continued living what he believed was the high life. Most nights his social activity revolved around alcohol, but during the day, Ken was at his desk, close to the ever consistent, ever hopeful, ever faithful Bill Morgan. Day after day he witnessed Bill's rock solid life. Periodically, Bill invited Ken to church and attempted to discuss the obvious problem Ken faced.

Finally, three years after his accident, Ken admitted to himself that he was sick. He knew he needed a different set of friends. He met a Christian girl and invited her to dinner.

Ken was excited because he sensed a new direction in his social life. A turning point in his life did occur the night of their date but for a reason that shocked Ken. You see, he had already decided he would not drink on the date because he knew his date was not prone to drink. Yet when the waiter stopped at their table, Ken's date quickly ordered herself a drink. Ken was shocked and immediately realized the impact of his discouraging life. His date drank that night because Ken's reputation had preceded him. Not only was his lifestyle going to kill him, Ken was going to take others down with him.

Ken reflected on the Morgans' lives. They were there for him the night of the wreck. They cared for him in the weeks following the accident. Bill confronted Ken in a spirit of kindness and gentleness while at the office. Through it all, Bill and Millie never wavered in their beliefs. As Ken later told me, "I always knew he was a good Christian man." On January 4, 1986, Ken Sawyer gave up the bottle and recommitted his life to Christ.

Without Bill and Millie Morgan, Ken Sawyer might not be with us today. They intervened in Ken's life. It would have been easy for Bill the employer to cast his eyes on other employees whose failings were less apparent, easier to deal with, and more socially accepted than those of Ken's, which were staring Bill in the face. Bill could have reasoned, "Heck, I could get sued. Anyway, if we are successful in getting Ken into treatment, my insurance premiums will skyrocket!" Fortunately, Ken Sawyer worked for an intervenor who was also an encourager.

Encouragement is an action, and a Christlike encourager is compelled to act or intervene in a needy person's life. Sometimes encouragement is impulsive, spur of the moment. Other times encouragement is intentional, following a godly plan of readiness resulting from our spiritual discipline and God's prompting. But all acts of encouragement are interventions into the routine or crisis of someone in need. The purpose of our encouraging interventions is change toward Christ. We intervene with the encouraging message of Christ so God can change the target of our action.

Barnabas—God's Encourager

Christ intends for His people to be intervenors. We are to be agents of change in other lives. Bill and Millie Morgan are beautiful examples of modern-day agents of change. The Bible tells about another change agent—an intervenor with an encouraging word about eternity. His name was Barnabas, and he is described in Scripture as "a good man, full of the Holy Spirit and faith" (Acts 11:24). This description of this son of encouragement is simple, but I believe it fully describes the characteristics necessary to intervene in the name of Christ.

Good

Barnabas was a good man. He was committed to moral and spiritual purity. His life was defined by the values of Christ which he held in his heart. The practice of Barnabas's life grew out of these values and resulted in a person who stood in contrast to those around him. This noticeable difference compelled his neighbors and those who encountered him to regard Barnabas as a good man.

Barnabas's reputation was credible, and he was in good standing in his community. It is from this platform of goodwill that Barnabas launched his ministry.

If you are interested in capturing your workplace for Christ, then you too must build a platform solid enough to launch your ministry. Imagine the reputation Barnabas would have earned if he were known to cheat his employer by arriving late to work on a regular basis. What if Barnabas bawled out his coworkers on occasion? I doubt that he would have been known as a good man if the actions of his life were contrary to the principles Christ taught.

If we are to be agents of change on Christ's behalf, we must believe and behave in a consistently different manner as compared to the rest of the world. We must first invite Christ to occupy His rightful place in our soul, and then, with laser beam intensity, we must focus on incorporating the values Christ modeled into our every action.

Bill and Millie Morgan understand the connection between a credible reputation and a successful intervention in a person's life. The Morgans' consistent, Christlike lives appealed to Ken Sawyer.

Ken knew Bill Morgan was a "good man." As a result of Bill's life and reputation, Ken accepted the intervention of God's change agent.

Spirit-Filled

Barnabas was also described as a man "full of the Holy Spirit." Have you met a person firmly under the direction of the Holy Spirit? It is usually obvious. A special empowering and boldness radiates from such a person's countenance and speech. An undeniable zeal coupled with a hair-trigger affirmative response to any opportunity of service marks a life directed by the Holy Spirit.

True eternal change comes only through Christ. Therefore an encouraging agent of true change must be driven by Christ through the Holy Spirit. We must submit to the authority and control of the Holy Spirit and operate out of His wisdom, His power, and His timing. Barnabas jumped at the opportunity to befriend and encourage Saul. He unhesitatingly encouraged Saul in specific circumstances under the control of the Holy Spirit.

Our modern-day sons of encouragement, Bill and Millie Morgan, submitted to the authority and control of the Holy Spirit. Through the Spirit's prompting, Bill and Millie saw Ken's need. Empowered by the Spirit, the Morgans intervened and encouraged Ken to change.

Millie and Bill recognized that an effective agent of true change was powerless without the indwelling of the Holy Spirit. If you desire to affect meaningful and lasting change in your workplace, you must invite the Holy Spirit to fill your heart and soul and direct your way.

Full of Faith

Barnabas's strong conviction influenced his eternal view of the future. It was the eternal nature of his outlook that compelled him to intervene in the life of Saul. How could Barnabas pass up the opportunity to encourage Saul through his eternally significant change? Barnabas saw that Saul was a man with enormous potential for the Kingdom. It was unthinkable that he would allow Saul's less-than-honorable past to prohibit Saul from realizing the eternal plan God had for his life.

Faith says God has a terrific plan for all of us. Faith believes that all believers are destined for a place that is greater than any thing or any place imaginable. Faith holds fast to the knowledge that God is in control.

Faith believes that with God anything is possible, including the conversion of the most feared antagonist of the early Christians. It was faith that held Bill and Millie Morgan to the belief that God could and would change Ken. Faith is the fuel of an encouraging intervention.

God desires to use you as one of His encouraging intervenors. If you think you are not up to the task, perhaps God is revealing areas in your life that need to be turned over to Him. It could be actions or events you consider insignificant. Gossiping, a poor work ethic, or unconfessed sin may be haunting you. If so, do not take this prompting as coincidence. The Holy Spirit is convicting you to get your life straight before God. Do it now! Then, realize that the qualifications of a godly change agent do not include formal religious training. Remember the description of Barnabas: "a good man, full of the Holy Spirit and faith." I do not see a seminary degree or the title of "reverend" in this description. God simply looks for His people to live a life changed by His grace and compelled to intervene in the changing of others for eternity. In the words of James, "In the same way, faith by itself, if it is not accompanied by action, is dead" (2:17).

The Impulsive Encourager

You may have started this chapter wondering why I devote an entire chapter to the value of encouragement. Perhaps you pictured a scene at your place of employment when someone encouraged you saying, "Great idea this morning," as you met in the hall. Maybe your mind scrolled back to the elevator encounter where a coworker told you to "have a nice day." While these words are encouraging, they are the product of impulse encouragement. Impulse encouragement occurs when the encourager, having given little if any advanced thought to his words, encounters someone and suddenly utters a kind phrase and a smile or a pat on the back. Once the parties depart, little if any thought is given to the encounter.

Impulse encouragement is like the first blast of fresh water pulsating from your morning shower. It is startling and refreshing, but the effect of its touch subsides quickly. The impulsive word of encouragement is helpful and nice for a moment, but very soon this form of encouragement rests in the "fond memory" file of our minds.

There is a place for this type of encouragement. I am an impulse encourager, and I challenge you to occasionally offer a kind word or a meaningful pat on the back to your coworkers. However, I believe God has a longer-lasting purpose for this godly trait of encouragement. I believe God desires for us to be not only impulse encouragers but also intentional encouragers.

The Intentional Encourager

Intentional encouragement is the result of a believer seeing a need for change in the life of another and intentionally and methodically intervening with encouragement for the purpose of affecting meaningful and eternal change. Encouraging interventions that are intentional are designed to permanently brand a needful person with the mark of Christ. Permanence in Christ is the purpose of any intentional encouraging intervention.

Maybe there are those in your work world who do not know Christ. Perhaps there are persons who have regressed in their walk with God. These people need encouragement *to* change. Others in your company may have recently accepted Christ or recommitted their lives to Him. They need encouragement *through* change. The remaining members of your eight-to-five team may be walking, even running, with Christ. They need encouragement to *maintain* change.

Anne Maddox grew up in a home of privilege. Her family was quite wealthy, affording Anne and her kin a lavish lifestyle. But while Anne was rich in the eyes of man, she was ridiculously poor in the sight of God. So poor, in fact, that she had never felt a need to pursue God—she had always been self-sufficient. Anne believed her life was without need, although really her life was without purpose.

Anne's insensitivity to God increased during her college days. Certain philosophy courses and a strong New Age message on campus drew her deeper into the foolish belief of self-sufficiency. Law school was a breeze, awarding her many honors and opportunities. By graduation, Anne's heart was more than insensitive to God—it was as hard as concrete.

Anne accepted a position with a large, prestigious law firm. One of the first people she met was Jennifer Adams, a paralegal. Jennifer was assigned to work for Anne. The two became fast friends and worked well as a team. Their workdays were demanding, often extending into the night. Sometimes they would go for a late dinner together.

When you work closely with someone, you usually get to know them quite well. For instance, Jennifer knew Anne was well traveled because of her stories about the many exotic destinations she had enjoyed. The two shared some common interests such as cycling and tennis, and they discussed their passion for both on occasion. But the subject of Christ and His church was never discussed, and Jennifer, a committed Christian and church member, grew increasingly aware of Anne's lack of faith.

Jennifer had never verbally confronted another person with the gospel. She was a good, moral person and served her church in several capacities, but she had never felt confident enough in her ability to say the right words to witness to an unbeliever. Frankly, Jennifer was scared.

One day, Anne saw a church flyer on Jennifer's desk advertising an upcoming event. "What's this?" Anne inquired. "Oh, we are having a guest speaker at my church this Sunday," Jennifer responded, without taking a breath. "Would you like to come?" Her mind danced with fresh energy. Unexpectedly, the ice had been broken with Anne. Surely, Jennifer thought, Anne will come and hear the message of Christ. "Never seen much point to all of that," answered Anne.

Jennifer fell into her chair, deflated by the encounter. Now she knew at least two sobering truths. First, Anne did not believe in Christ, and second, Jennifer was not going to be able to pass the responsibility of witnessing to Anne onto someone else. Jennifer knew Anne needed to change. The encouraging intervention had begun, and from this point forward the effort must be intentional.

Jennifer called on the Holy Spirit to give her new boldness and the right words to confront Anne. Jennifer purposed to become a change agent for the Creator, believing everlasting change would occur in Anne's life. Day after day Jennifer prayed for opportunities to share Christ. However, it seemed the more Jennifer prayed, the more distant Anne became.

Soon Anne began to challenge Jennifer's work. She questioned its accuracy and timeliness. Jennifer was required to report to work earlier and stay later. Anne intensified the pressure on Jennifer, who continued to pray for her boss. In time, Jennifer discerned the reason for Anne's increasing intensity and viewed it as an opportunity to witness.

Jennifer had something different, something special—and Anne wanted it. Anne had seen a unique spark in Jennifer's life from the first day on the job. The flyer on Jennifer's desk and her invitation to church clued Anne as to the source of her paralegal's uncommon life. It was God, and He was one Person Anne had never needed— or so she thought—until now.

So untenable was the thought that Anne needed God and was, therefore, no longer self-sufficient that she purposed to prove God really does not make a difference. Her ploy? Drive Jennifer to the breaking point and wait for her to reach out to something or somebody other than Christ. That would prove that Christ is not the answer, and Anne would have no need to change.

The only problem was that Anne was dead wrong. Jennifer held the truth in her heart, and the Holy Spirit ministered to her by emboldening her with new confidence and an unquestionable command of her beliefs. When we seek to encourage others to change, we must remain confident and hold a strong command of our beliefs. The person we are encouraging to change will find comfort in our confidence and conviction in our beliefs.

Are You an Encourager?

You may identify with Jennifer. Maybe a coworker is lost, and although you feel compelled to witness to that needful person, the fear of speaking up is overwhelming. Perhaps you are afraid that your intervention in his life, however encouraging, may be harmful to the cause. Perhaps the object of your concern is your boss, and you feel an intervention on your part will negatively effect your career.

If so, relax. Be confident in the Lord, just as Bill and Millie Morgan were and just as Jennifer learned to be. Paul exhorted the Philippians, "Let your gentleness be evident to all. The Lord is near. Do not be anxious about anything, but in everything, by prayer and petition, with thanksgiving, present your requests to God" (Phil. 4:5–6). The Lord is with you, so do not fret over things we as human beings cannot control—such as another's decision to accept Christ. The ultimate decision to believe in Christ is between each person and God. You must pray that God will reveal opportunities for intervention and soften the heart of your friend in need.

Paul also gives us the promise of acting on this Scripture, "And the peace of God, which transcends all understanding, will guard your hearts and your minds in Christ Jesus" (Phil. 4:7). We can be confident in our intervention because God will protect our hearts and minds, producing an inner tranquillity that is impossible to comprehend unless you are its beneficiary.

The pressure is gone. Our role in an encouraging intervention in the lives of others who need to begin change is to remain sensitive to the needs around us and then, with confidence and a command of our beliefs, to step forward boldly.

The end result is up to God and your needful friend.

Anne continued to heap piles of work on Jennifer and demanded more of her time at work. Through it all, Jennifer prayed, worked to meet the challenges presented by Anne, and took advantage of opportunities to talk with her boss about Christ. One evening Jennifer returned to the office to find Anne, face down at her desk, sobbing. This lawyer that had it all found that "it" was not enough. With a sense of relief, Anne turned to Jennifer for help. Jennifer's constancy during those difficult days was used by the Holy Spirit to soften Anne's hardened heart. That evening in her office, Anne accepted the grace of Jesus Christ. Her heart was changed. Anne knew that now—at last—she truly had it all.

❖ What is your scriptural I.Q.? Do you know the scriptural basis of your belief in Christ? If not, ask your pastor for assistance.

❖ One test of your scriptural I.Q. is your confidence in sharing your belief in Christ. Are you confident when you share your testimony? If not, begin a study of the Scriptures to understand and learn the facts of your faith.

Encouraging a New Christian

Encouraging people to see their need for change and working with them to affect change is only one aspect of our responsibility as God's change agents. Once a person accepts Christ, radical change unfolds in his or her life. We must be prepared to encourage the convert through these changes.

The first days of life as a new Christian can be frightening. Shedding the ritual and rut of our past is difficult, and that process can be complicated if our old associates do not support our decision. Giving expressions of high value and communicating the importance of the future with Christ are essential when intervening to encourage someone through change.

Few of us have experienced an intervention such as the Damascus Road dialogue between God and Saul. Soon after Saul's conversion he began preaching in the synagogues. After about three years the Jews conspired to kill him. Fearing for his life, Saul escaped to Jerusalem in search of the disciples, for surely they would accept and protect him. But that was not the case. The disciples were afraid of Saul and doubted the sincerity of his conversion.

Then Barnabas encouragingly intervened. "Barnabas took him and brought him to the apostles. He told them how Saul on his journey had seen the Lord and that the Lord had spoken to him, and how in Damascus he had preached fearlessly in the name of the Jesus" (Acts 9:27). What an incredible expression of high value! Barnabas stood shoulder to shoulder with the man who helped kill one of their own, Stephen, and advocated his admission to the group. Why? Barnabas knew throwing Saul out on his own could seriously damage the good that Christ had brought about in Saul's life already, not to mention the potential of the future work of Saul.

In your salt mine there are persons who are struggling through change of an eternal nature. Some of your coworkers may be new Christians, while others may be backslidden believers on the mend. These brothers and sisters in Christ need your expressions of high value. They need to feel your acceptance each day. They need you to stand shoulder to shoulder with them as they work to overcome the past.

Jason's Encourager

Jason had been married twice before. He had a son from one of the unions. Now he was headed down the aisle again, and word circulated that he had known his bride-to-be only three months. His coworkers were unmerciful in their comments. When he added that this marriage was different because Christ was the center of both of their lives, the gathering of coworkers broke up in laughter.

Jason was new to the faith and unaccustomed to ridicule. He was getting a crash course from his self-appointed instructors when Steve stepped in. Steve was highly respected by his peers because of his tenure and the quality of his work. His words extinguished the group's fiery rhetoric like water from a fireman's pump truck. He said, "Jason is a good man who recently accepted Christ. Christ makes a huge difference. I know because of the difference Christ has made in my life. Like Jason and all of you, I have made mistakes in the past, but Christ has forgiven me and cleared my path for a bright future. Can all of you say that?" Class dismissed. Jason straightened his back and thanked Steve for his encouraging intervention.

❖ How do you express your feelings of high value for someone? Maybe you are known as an encourager at home or at church, but it has never occurred to you to be an encourager at work. Utilize your gift at work. Perhaps you express high value through the spoken word or through some form of hospitality. Purpose to show at least one person at work his or her value to you and Christ today.

❖ Look for the new Christians around you. Do not neglect the opportunity to tell them of the glorious future to be realized through their daily walk with Christ.

Encouraging Others to Stay on Track

Our world is full of distractions and pitfalls. Today, many avenues exist that, if taken, lead to destruction. The same situation existed in Antioch when Barnabas arrived. There were cults masquerading as the real thing, promiscuity was on the rise, and public corruption was the norm.

Confronted by these facts of life, the church in Antioch began an evangelistic effort. The obedience of this young church was rewarded by the conversion of many people. Barnabas was dispatched to Antioch to check on their ministry. "When he arrived and saw the evidence of the grace of God, he was glad and encouraged them all to remain true to the Lord with all their hearts" (Acts 11:23).

The church at Antioch had been caught. They were caught in the act of doing the right thing, and Barnabas affirmed their work. All of us need affirmation to stay the course. We need to know that our endeavors are worthwhile and that our efforts are making a difference.

David's Case: Who Encourages the Encourager?

Catching others doing what is right and worthwhile in the eyes of the Savior is the first critical element to maintaining our Christlike growth pattern. David Randolph sought to capture his workplace for Christ. As the president of his company, David had wide latitude to install programs for the employees. With the help of some others, David initiated a program in his institution that was appropriately seasoned with the salty message of Christ. The employees gathered for the program's kick-off and seemed to accept David's instruction quite well. But for several weeks David did not hear any feedback on his efforts. Were people affected by this program? David did not know, and it was beginning to concern him.

One day David stepped onto the elevator and was greeted by one of his line workers. This single-parent mom spoke to David saying, "I was thinking about what you said a few weeks ago. Your testimony has made a huge difference in my life. Thanks!" Wow! The elevator headed down, but David's heart blasted heavenward. Here was affirmation that his teaching was solid and making a difference. Interestingly, most days when David begins to question the impact of the program, he receives a note or a call or a simple word from someone on the elevator detailing an event or area of that person's life that has changed. David, who acted as an encouraging intervenor himself, is the recipient of such interventions also.

Encouraging Others to Take Responsibility

A second necessary element of a successful intervention is encouragement to take responsibility. Now solidly on Christ's flight path, persons should look for opportunities to serve. As Christ's change agent, you should assist other believers in their efforts to capture their workplaces for Christ by suggesting areas where needs exist and Christlike service would make a difference.

Remember Ken Sawyer? Well, he continued on the growth path. Along the way Bill and Millie and others showed expressions of high value for Ken both privately and publicly. He was constantly reminded of his important future. Bill Morgan caught Ken doing the right thing a lot.

Yearning for more, Ken was encouraged to lead a Bible study. Eventually he and his wife Leah led a number of studies, involving many people from Ken's office. Ken and Leah also took responsibility for a Sunday school class at their church.

My pastor, Jay Wolf, says, "The fruit is out on the limb." He uses this word picture to teach an important truth: the juicy fruit of joyous service for Christ is found when we step out into an area where God, and God alone, can bring about change in us. Being "out on the limb" is often uncomfortable—and risky. We have left the familiarity and strength of the trunk behind. We are vulnerable and weak and unsteady. Yet in this weakened condition, God can use us, and we must acknowledge His working because we know the good harvest was not of our hand. It is our limblike experiences that feed our growth.

Do not be misled by the word *maintain* as it relates to the purpose of encouragement. Ongoing growth is the experience of the Christian. Therefore, *maintaining* your eternal change means that you keep on growing.

❖ Open your eyes to the work of those around you. Focus on the newer Christians in your midst. Do not miss their Christlike actions. Catch them doing the Christlike thing, and encourage them.

❖ Help find your Christian coworkers' eternal work. Include them in your efforts to capture your workplace for Christ. Help them identify opportunities in their churches where they can take responsibility.

The Promise of Encouragement

Why bother? Why take the time and energy to intervene in someone's life with encouragement to change for eternity? First, if you are a believer in Jesus Christ, then someone brought the encouraging message of the Savior to you. It may have been your parents or a friend or even a coworker. But the message of the Lord came to you through one of God's agents of change. Are you angry at the one that loved you enough to tell you the truth? I doubt it. Go and do likewise.

The second compelling reason to offer encouragement is that Christ commanded us to intervene. You will hear this from me over and over, and I do not apologize for the repetition. God said it, so it bears repeating: "Therefore go and make disciples" (Matt. 28:19).

What is the promise of an encouraging intervention? Earlier in this chapter we discussed the characteristics of a godly change agent, specifically Barnabas. The description of Barnabas goes on to say, "A great number of people were brought to the Lord" (Acts 11:24). You may never know the effect of your efforts on behalf of Christ until you meet Him face to face. You may have to wait until that day to see the lives that were changed as a result of your obedience to the Father, but you can be sure that the Holy Spirit is using your intentional efforts to impact the lives of others. You must be confident that you will be for someone else what Bill Morgan was for Ken Sawyer.

We have a saying in our church: "Bring them in, build them up, and send them out." By this we mean that we must lead others to Christ, disciple them, and then empower them for service. This is the essence of our role as godly agents of change; it is our mission. Encouragement should produce change. Purposeful change. Eternal change.

3

Forgiveness
From Failure to Freedom

Too often we think that forgiveness is an old-fashioned value that has no place in today's workplace. On the contrary, forgiveness can actually improve productivity in the workplace.

The Unforgiving Workplace

Zero Defects

"Zero Defects" was the message on the signs plastered like wallpaper around the meeting hall. The president of this mid-sized company proudly unveiled the coming year's theme to a crowd of expectant stockholders. "This year we will demand that our people produce products with zero defects. We will tolerate nothing less!" the CEO announced to a swooning constituency. The die was cast.

Alice Heath worked as a financial analyst for this manufacturer of home products. She was well known throughout the organization due to her twenty-two-year tenure. Alice started her career with the company as an administrative assistant to the president. (Yes, the same president who committed his troops to the unrealistic and, frankly, unattainable goal of zero defects.) As opportunities opened in the company, Alice advanced, always growing in her knowledge and ability.

Alice liked her current job as financial analyst in the acquisitions department. She traveled extensively, analyzing potential companies and making recommendations to senior management regarding any action the company should take.

Soon after the annual stockholders meeting Alice was dispatched to analyze a firm that made a competing product. The due-diligence checklist was carved into her mind, the result of dozens of visits to targeted firms. Alice crunched numbers, interviewed personnel, and reviewed files and policies. After a week or so, the on-site visit was complete, and Alice returned home to draft her findings.

The top brass considered Alice Heath an all-star. Heath-led acquisitions completed by her department had all performed well. Maybe it was the confidence she had built in her ability that compelled Alice to conduct her review of this current target company using only the checklist in her memory. As a result, for the first time in her stellar tenure, material information was omitted from her report—information so sensitive that had Alice uncovered it, she may have recommended against acquiring the company. However, unwittingly, Alice recommended the purchase. Her employer followed her advice, closing the transaction in just a few months.

The newly merged companies performed well by every measure. Earnings were strong and growing fueled in large part by the increased productivity of the combined workforce. Sales also grew, with new customers contributing to the increase.

#@*~!

About mid-morning on a cold January day, Alice was summoned to her boss's office. There was a tone in his voice that warned Alice of a coming firestorm. When she entered his corner sanctuary, a barrage of verbal missiles hit her: "Tell me why I shouldn't fire you right now!" he yelled. "You are the lousiest excuse for an analyst I have ever seen. You #@*~!" Alice attempted to calm him down, but he just responded, "I'm Mr. Smith to you!" She had worked with this superior for fifteen years, and they had been on a first name basis for most of that time. His attempt to demean Alice went on for another twenty minutes.

Alice made one mistake in a zero-defects workplace. During her visit to the acquisition candidate, Alice had forgotten to find out if anyone was suing the company. Unfortunately, her manager learned there was a class action lawsuit against their new subsidiary. The ultimate effect of the suit was still unclear, but the fact remained that Alice had missed the litigation. Her years of hard work and her exemplary record were forgotten. Alice had made a mistake.

She felt terrible. She apologized and offered to do anything possible to rectify the omission. She even offered to go to the president and tell him of her mistake. Alice tried to focus on ways to improve the current situation as well as future due-diligence visits. But much to her surprise, there would be no future due-diligence visits. In fact, for Alice, there would be no future with her longtime employer at all. Her boss curtly stated that he "could not forgive" her for this gross negligence and wanted her out of the building by noon.

Goals and the Human Equation

Zero defects. Such a policy might work well with machines, but it has no place with people. Since Adam and Eve, we have been inherently fallible souls. I have yet to meet anyone that meets the standard of perfection of our Savior. Alice certainly was prone to error, as we all are. Forgiveness lubricates our cranky relationships and squeaky performance on the job.

I believe you need only to reflect on today's workday to visualize a situation in need of forgiveness. A coworker betrayed your confidence. Your boss treated you unkindly. Perhaps you are the one in need of the grace of a forgiving spirit. Opportunities to capture our workplaces for Christ through forgiveness are many. But these occasions too often slip through our fingers.

The story of Alice Heath is repeated day after day in workplaces everywhere. Stress builds as demands increase. Most workers strive to meet goals such as increased sales growth and increased earnings per share. Although these are worthy goals, performance objectives sometimes get out of perspective. Too often the pressure to meet these goals consumes us, and we forsake the highest calling of our labor-honoring God through our work and enlarging His kingdom.

The Classic Workplace Response

Unfortunately, participants in the workworld today routinely respond to errors, mistakes, and bungled relationships in an angry, unhealthy, and unchristian manner. If Alice and all the Alicelike workers make a mistake, then they must pay for it. If a coworker trips in his relationship with another, then he should pay somehow. An eye-for-eye/tooth-for-tooth mindset seems to rule our lives from eight to five. This anger blocks our willingness to forgive.

You may be motivated by the possibility of teaching the principle of forgiveness to your unbelieving coworker, but before you hold the first class, take a look around. If your workplace is like most, then you need to invite many of your fellow Christians. Many believers, who on Sunday are living images of Christ, awaken Monday morning and peer into a different mirror. They see a different image, and they believe that an ungodly weekday image is acceptable.

Many Christians believe an angry and unforgiving spirit is acceptable in "the real world" of work. How many times have we heard someone say, "You had better let them know who is boss. It is good to show your temper. You can always come around later and smooth things over. Anyway, Christ showed His anger when He threw people out of the temple. If He yelled at people, why shouldn't we?"

You may have had a boss or coworker use such an argument to tempt you to operate the world's way. I encourage you to look up the account of Jesus in the temple (Luke 19:45–48). You will not find a single reference to Jesus being angry as He tossed the money-changers out of His temple. Furthermore, can we even compare an error or mistake made at work, whether careless or intentional, to the desecration of God's temple? Any modern-day error pales in importance when compared to an attack on the Holy of Holies.

Anger and forgiveness are foes. It is as impossible for an angry person to forgive as it is for a forgiving person to harbor anger. Anger is a sin, a manifestation of our old self. Believers are admonished to deal with their angry hearts. "Put off all these: anger, wrath, malice" (Col. 3:8, KJV).

Perhaps you are a believer having a difficult time shaking the bondage of anger. So did I. When I was about twelve years old my temper was as quick as microwave popcorn. In a matter of seconds, my demeanor could jettison from a calm, happy child to that of a raging bull. My angry outbursts were so serious that my parents and my older brother and sister had to hold me down under a blanket until calm was restored.

Then one day, the Man who calmed the raging seas added my angry heart to His list of miraculous accomplishments. Even though a child, I knew my anger was inappropriate, so I prayed that God would deliver me from its snare. We serve a God who answers prayers. He answered mine, and He will answer yours as well. If you are held captive by the sin of anger, recognize its source and call on God, our Overcomer.

What's more, if you are serious about capturing your company for Christ, you must root out any anger that may be moored to your heart so that you can forgive and forget. Regardless of your position on the company ladder, your anger is unjustified; you have no right to cruise around your job site like a great white shark looking for the next victim.

Disassociation

Following an outburst of anger, many people employ a tactic of disassociation by either ostracizing or terminating the employee. Disassociation follows anger as a favorite tool of the one who refuses to forgive.

Ostracized

Janice received orders from the director's office at the state capitol. The orders read, "You are hereby transferred to field office 3." The director might as well have transferred Janice to Siberia. Field offices were not a springboard to promotion, especially not field office 3. Adding to the insult was Janice's diminished role within the agency.

The news was upsetting to Janice, but not totally unexpected. The director (I will call him Robert) was known to respond swiftly and harshly to anyone questioning policy.

Several years earlier, the director made a policy decision regarding the use of overtime. In a nutshell, this state agency converted all hourly workers to a salary. The director believed that if employees were salaried then they were exempt from being paid overtime. Robert then instituted a hiring freeze. As most governmental agencies do, this division of state government grew in its scope. More work distributed over the same number of employees necessarily meant more hours worked, but the new overtime policy meant the employees of that agency did not receive overtime pay.

Janice held a position of responsibility. She would not have been eligible for overtime even if the department paid it. Yet, Janice was concerned for the rank and file employees, and she knew from prior work experience that the policy was flawed. So a memo from Janice outlining her understanding of the Fair Labor Standards Act and requesting a meeting on the subject was distributed to the director, several top managers in the agency, and the state personnel director.

Robert was not amused. His secret was out, thanks to Janice. Now he and his poor policymaking was in the spotlight. Robert, in turn, made sure Janice would not be in any future spotlight. He ostracized her to field office 3, where Janice would be out of sight and out of mind.

Some managers think Robert's response was justified, even noble. They argue that Janice should have been fired but was spared because of the director's benevolence. Robert went home the day of the transfer proud of his compassion, while Janice withdrew crushed.

Termination

Termination is the other tool of disassociation, the one Alice Heath knows well. She made one mistake and got the boot. There are circumstances where termination is the best course of action, but overlooking something important does not always fall into that category. In today's high-stress culture, managers sometimes cave in to the pressure of the moment. As a result, they may ostracize or terminate an employee.

If you think all this applies only to managers, think again! Anger and disassociation also creep in among production-line workers. If you work and interact with anyone on your job, then there is a powerful message here for you.

When a coworker stumbles, and you are the affected party, how do you respond? When was the last time a coworker let you down? Did you get angry? Did you try to wound the perpetrator with a harsh glance and an unredeeming word? Did you storm off kicking and screaming, vowing not to speak to the person again? If so, you showed everyone your old self. You went public with your struggle with sin. You showed them your need for forgiveness.

Thankfully, we serve a God of hope and forgiveness who will never forsake us. He stays with us even when we fall and dishonor Him. Like a loving father, our God picks us up, dusts us off, and sends us back into the battle of life with a clean slate. If you are intent on capturing your company for Christ, you must follow the example of our Redeemer—forgive and forget.

Fleshing Out Forgiveness

Most days, circuit court Judge Jim Guthrey can be found in his court listening to the stories of countless criminal defendants. It is Judge Guthrey's awesome task to decide the fate of people who have failed. While his coworkers are relatively few, this judge and all judges have a wide-ranging influence. Judge Guthrey is transforming his work-world for Christ.

I had the bittersweet opportunity to witness Judge Guthrey in action. Two friends of mine finished a round of golf and a case of beer at a nearby course. On their way home, the curves in the two-lane road proved too difficult for my intoxicated friends. They crashed. Al was seated in the passenger's seat, and he was killed instantly. Berry was driving, but he survived. Berry was charged with vehicular homicide, and his case was assigned to Judge Guthrey.

An agreement was reached, and Berry plead guilty to manslaughter. March 17, 1995, was the date Judge Guthrey set for the sentencing. I was there, and I will never forget what happened. Emotions were high as about fifty of us piled into the courtroom. The odds of escaping time in jail were not in Berry's favor. Judge

Guthrey was tough on criminal defendants; he had never before sentenced someone to probation when alcohol had caused a death.

The proceeding started in the usual way, but the judge cut to the meat of the matter very quickly. Hearts were pounding as the judge began his remarks. Berry's attorneys spoke on his behalf. Several people in the gallery addressed the court. Then the most remarkable and memorable words were uttered by Al's father.

"Judge, I hate that we are here today. We are here because my son was killed, and he should be alive. But Judge, I have come today to represent Al and to speak on behalf of Berry. Judge, we have forgiven Berry and Al." At this point in the grieving father's monologue, tears were flowing like the Colorado River. Even Judge Guthrey wept. Al's father continued to plead for Berry and closed by asking for leniency.

The judge was moved by the dad's Christlike display of forgiveness. The five-year sentence imposed by the court was suspended a moment later. Berry was placed on probation with the condition and understanding that one ounce or more of alcohol imbibed by Berry would be an automatic ticket to jail.

Then Judge Guthrey intervened in Berry's life directly, saying, "Berry, you must seek forgiveness and get on with your life." Pointing to the man who had lost his son in the senseless accident, the judge said, "This man needs a son. Would you be his son, Berry? And sir, would you accept him?" The gallery was beyond tears. Wailing is more descriptive of the scene.

Powerfully and appropriately the father of a son killed in an unnecessary circumstance taught an incredible lesson about forgiveness. Judge Guthrey followed the forgiving father by communicating the worth of the one forgiven. "Would you be his son, Berry? You are worthy, Berry. You have a future, Berry. You can do great things, Berry, now that you are unshackled from the bondage of this tragedy." Anger and disassociation gave way to forgiveness.

Judge Guthrey and Al's dad are uncommon in our world. Most dads would have asked for the electric chair, and most judges would have played to the emotions of a voting community rather than sincerely looking at the hearts of those affected and rendering a fair decision.

At first glance this story may not appear to be relevant to your workworld. But in any circumstance you may be cast as the offender (Berry) or the victim (Al's dad) or the objective third party (Judge Guthrey). Are you ready to forgive? Your opportunity to capture your workplace for Christ depends on it.

So, what about it? In your week of work how did you respond to the hurt and disappointment of the failings of others? The time has come for believers to absorb the pain of our own and others' failures and, with the help of Christ, offer forgiveness to the unforgivable. Put off anger and disassociation, and follow the teachings of our forgiving God.

Our Savior looked to the criminal on the next cross and offered His forgiveness. Jesus peered down from His painful platform and forgave all of us who put Him to death. As believers, we should follow the example of Christ and forgive.

Four Steps to Forgiveness

"Get real!" you say. "When a coworker slams me in the presence of my boss, am I really supposed to forgive him? If so, how?" Maybe your boss considers yelling at his employees great sport. Is he due your forgiveness? In a word, *yes*. And I believe the Scriptures offer inspired teaching on how we can forgive even the most difficult people.

Step 1: See Others from God's Perspective

The first step to forgiveness is seeing your coworkers from God's perspective. Take your eyes off the offender and look up to the Savior. Jesus sees each of us as eternally significant beings with brilliant potential. God's vantage point teaches that we have all sinned and that we are all helpless without the blood of Christ.

This admonition to look through godly lenses is tough when a fellow laborer steps on us to get ahead. Looking around our workplace with godly eyes is difficult if we have been displaced for no good reason. Yet over and over we see how Christ responded to the scorn of others with compassion and forgiveness. "When he saw the crowds, he had compassion on them, because they were harassed and helpless, like sheep without a shepherd" (Matt. 9:36).

You may work with people whose lives are defined in that verse—helpless and harassed, sheep without a shepherd, aimlessly meandering from one day to the next. It is little wonder that many of your coworkers suffer from debilitating anger, an unforgiving spirit, and a me-first attitude.

It is for these souls that we seek to capture our workplaces for Christ. Our human perspective on the person at the next desk or in the next office or on the next line is not good enough. We must seek the perfect perspective, the forgiving perspective of the Creator of us all. Judge Guthrey views his coworkers and courtroom participants through God's eyes. The result for Berry was an appropriate decision that affirmed his worth to God.

Gaining a godly perspective comes as a result of the discipline of prayer. Christ instructs us to "pray for those who persecute you" (Matt. 5:44). Do we pray to inform God of someone's misconduct so He can wipe them out? Of course not. We pray so God will change us and hone us more to His image.

Intelligence agencies use satellites to transmit messages and images around the world. A message may be sent from Washington to Moscow via satellite. Imagine a drawing of the process. A line would run between the sender and the satellite resulting in another line between the satellite and the receiver. The message is sent in English, but it is received in Russian.

Prayer is our spiritual satellite system. We voice our concerns, fears, apologies, and requests to God, and He beams back His perspective and will for us. God will take our finite, human perspective on another's life and miraculously transform it into a Christ-honoring, selfless, forgiving spirit. Through prayer we gain God's perspective.

Step 2: Leave the Offense at the Cross

Prayer also carries us back to the Cross. It allows us to leave the offense at the Cross, once and for all.

Judge Guthrey told Berry to leave his offense at the foot of the Cross. He encouraged Berry to forgive himself and to seek others' forgiveness for his failure. Then the judge told Berry to get on with his life, to put this event behind him. The charge from the bench was to leave the yoke of this crime at the Cross of the One who already paid the price!

Have you been the victim of a coworker's mistake? Have you said to yourself, "Every dog has his day. My day is coming." That is the easy response. The Bible describes a different response: "Be kind and compassionate to one another, forgiving each other, just as in Christ God forgave you" (Eph. 4:32). What is your pain compared to the pain Christ endured on your behalf?

Alice, Janice, and Al's dad could have held grudges, and their colleagues would have supported them. Yet in all three cases they applied the oil of forgiveness, and each one found their go gear in short order. Forgiving someone is energizing and often helps the victim as much as it does the offender. Leaving the offense at the foot of the Cross is liberating, and from that act pours forth a geyser of joy.

Maybe you identify with the quick-tempered bosses. Maybe Berry's story strikes a familiar chord. If forgiveness is offered, you, too, will enjoy its energy and liberation. But do not wait for the target of your mistake to seek you out. The ball is in your court. Go to the hurting party and ask them to forgive you. Then forgive yourself and turn the memory over to Christ.

When Christ died on that cross, He created a lasting reminder of His loving forgiveness. If you are harboring the pain of a past wound, make a trip to the "dump for damaged feelings." Make a prayerful deposit, then put the memory out of your mind. Enjoy the peace and the joy.

Step 3: Operate Out of Your Will and Reason

The third step to responding with godly forgiveness is to operate out of your will and reason, not out of your emotions. After you have gained God's perspective and left the burden of your error at the Cross, then, with a reasonable heart, meet to discuss the error and the future.

The prophet Isaiah communicated to the people of Judah and Jerusalem God's dissatisfaction with their behavior. He related the wages of their sin and then announced a marvelous offer from God: "Come now, let us reason together, says the LORD" (Isa. 1:18). God asked the failing people of Judah and Jerusalem to come and talk about the situation rationally and with cool heads.

God has given humans a special ability to reason that distinguishes us from other creatures. But in the jungle of commerce we sometimes act like animals. Like the territorial lion, we quickly dispose of coworkers whose actions annoy us. With lightning speed we unleash our anger on the very ones in need of forgiveness.

Alice Heath worked for a group that did not respond to her error reasonably. Instead, her supervisor made a quick decision to terminate her. In the process he dismissed one of the brightest and best people in the company. The boss reacted out of his own emotion, not out of his reason and will. Janice, too, fell prey to the quick emotional response of one not sensitive to God's view.

In your Judah-like job locale you may have experienced the quick hand of a boss responding angrily, not reasonably. Maybe a coworker told a lie about you. These people need your forgiveness. Follow the instruction found in Isaiah and slow down. Calm down. Do not rush to judgment. Pray. Meet and discuss the conflict. Listen and reason. Forgive.

Step 4: Rebuild and Restore

Several months after Janice had been deep sixed in field office 3 she received a call from Robert, her boss. Robert requested a meeting at the field office. Janice could not imagine what the director could possibly want. She listened as Robert apologized for his earlier actions. Robert sought her forgiveness, though much to his surprise, Janice had already forgiven him soon after the incident.

A state employment system policy prohibited Janice from transferring from her downgraded position for nine more months, but the two coworkers agreed to meet on a regular basis and work to repair their relationship. Eventually, Janice shared her prayers with Robert and began to discuss Christ with him.

Restoration and rebuilding is what Christ is all about. He wastes neither anything nor anyone. Imagine the hurt you would feel if one of your closest friends betrayed you. Would you try to restore and rebuild your relationship with your betrayer? During the biggest crisis of Jesus' earthly life, Simon Peter denied knowing the Savior.

Did Jesus brood and hold a grudge? Did He exact vengeance on His fallen friend? No. Christ rose from the grave and embraced Peter. Jesus forgave His friend, and a hurting Simon Peter was rebuilt and restored.

Transforming your company for Christ can be a difficult task. It is possible only if you will humble yourself and seek and offer forgiveness. We must slow down and reason with godly wisdom. Seeing others from God's perspective, we should take our pain and the pain of others and leave it behind us at the Cross. Then we should look to the future as eternal builders and restore our broken relationships.

Take a minute to reflect on situations this week when you should have used forgiveness. Were you the victim, the offender, or the innocent bystander? Did you represent your Lord in a manner that would be pleasing to Him? What actions can you take in the next twenty-four hours to open the pathway to forgiveness?

Make a list of persons you need to forgive and persons from whom you need forgiveness. Begin praying for them today. Then

- ❖   see them from God's perspective,
- ❖   leave the offense at the cross,
- ❖   act out of reason, and
- ❖   restore and rebuild.

The Benefits of Forgiveness

Healthier Relationships

Janice followed the liberating path of forgiveness. She had responded calmly to Robert following the transfer notice. As she contemplated the unforeseen and hurtful events, Janice imagined how God might see her boss. She made a trip to the Cross, laid down her ill feelings, and walked away. Then, at the appropriate opportunity, she began to rebuild and restore her boss.

God honored her obedience. Janice's willingness to forgive and forget was so uncommon in Robert's world that he was overwhelmed by a desire to know the source of her strength. Robert and Janice continued to talk on a regular basis. They enjoyed one of the results of a forgiving spirit—an open and healthy relationship. Conversation grew from superficial chatter to life-changing dialog. Robert questioned Janice about her faith. The Holy Spirit softened his heart, and eventually, he accepted Christ.

Increased Creativity

At the moment Robert believed, he received the second result of forgiveness, the freedom to fail. In Christ our debt is paid regardless of our sin. The blood of Christ covered all of our sin. We only have to ask Him to forgive us and He honors our sincere requests.

Life around the state agency changed when Robert accepted the Savior. A new culture was born, a culture that allowed workers to fail and try again, a culture that eventually thrived on success because it allowed people to learn from their failures.

When you and I forgive others, when we commit to live the life modeled by Christ, nonbelievers can see Jesus. Forgiveness says, "You are worthy because of who you are and not because of what you do." Forgiveness says, "Zero Defects should be reserved for machines."

Forgiveness liberates us to enjoy healthy, open relationships. Forgiveness unleashes our creativity because we are free to fail.

4

Balance
Calibrated by Christ

The 1980s produced memorable characters—people like stock market manipulators Michael Milken, Ivan Bosky, and Charles Keating. These men were smart. They had families. And each of them had a consuming, overwhelming desire for wealth that preempted everything else. Their lives were not properly calibrated.

Milken, Bosky, and Keating were not the only people affected by the greed bug during the 1980s. Yes, I must admit that it was a decade of imbalance for me too. While I did not engage in illegal activity, I did buy into the mindset that building wealth has first priority.

The Bill Nix Story

Investment bankers travel much, if not most, of the time. I was no stranger to Atlanta's Hartsfield International Airport or other airports across the United States. I was away from my home and my family a lot.

A typical week for me during the eighties started on Monday morning at the Montgomery airport at 5:45 A.M. For the next few days I lived out of my suitcase and conducted business wherever I found a client. From southern California to central Ohio to Pittsburgh to Helsinki, Finland, I traveled wherever a client or qualified prospect had a deal to be done.

On days when I worked out of my office, I was at my desk by 7:00 A.M. The lights of my office did not dim until 6:00 P.M. or later. I even worked some Sundays. Nonetheless, I still questioned my commitment to the business after reading featured articles on Michael Milken's work habits.

No Vacation

Then there was the issue of vacations. I rarely took a day off. When I did retreat from the office, my brief case was always among the luggage. I was awestruck by the account of the Milken family vacation to Hawaii. It was reported that Milken rented two suites at the hotel. One suite was for his family and the other for his work. Since Hawaii is in a distant time zone, it was a perfect vacation spot for a workaholic like Milken. By day Milken could play with his family while the mainland slept, but when bedtime came in Hawaii, the forty-eight contiguous states were waking to a new day. Milken stayed up most of the night in his second suite communicating with his west coast office—doing deals and adding to his already enormous net worth. After two hours of sleep, Mike was ready to play again. I thought, *Wow! What a great vacation! How efficient!*

First and foremost, I was an investment banker. I took care of the needs of my clients, although I neglected my family's needs. I was either traveling far from home or out of the house before Teri, Lauren, Will, and Mary Grayson tumbled out of bed. When I was at home, my mind was still officebound.

May 5, 1988, is a day I will never forget. My son was born on that day. While Teri was in labor and delivery, I was in the hall on the phone laboring to make a deal work. I had instructed the nurses to let me know if Teri needed me or if she was ready to deliver. Periodically I bounced into her room, held her hand for a moment, then went back to my first priority. I was with her when Will was actually delivered, and I am forever thankful for that. But looking back, I cannot see why Teri put up with me.

No Time for God

My life with God was also out of balance. I accepted Christ when I was seven. My walk with Him grew during the seventies.

Then during the eighties my career took off and my priority shifted from my Savior to myself. My eternal life perspective, which was so evident in the seventies, gave way to the narrow and destructive view of the here and now. The peace and contentment I had known as a result of my properly balanced life vanished like a mist.

But God intervened. In joyous circumstances God often speaks to us in a whisper. In painful circumstances His speaking is as unmistakable as the roar of a train whistle. That is where God spoke to me. I was frozen in the headlight of an on-coming train of pain. Actually, He had been speaking to me since my selfish tour began. Only now, in the midst of a crisis, did I open my heart to listen.

"Your Father Has Cancer!"

My father had always been my best friend and my earthly mentor. One Friday evening, exactly one month after Will's birth, Teri and the kids picked me up at the airport. I hopped into the car and we talked for a moment. Then Teri spoke words that still echo in my mind: "Your dad went to the doctor today; they found spots on his lung." Cancer. "No way!" I responded. "He had polyps in his colon last year, and they were benign."

The next morning I hurried to my father's house and found him sitting in a dark den. This was very uncharacteristic. He was usually full of life and abounding with energy. His den was the place to watch live sporting events or a video of an Auburn football game. It was usually an active place—but not that day.

My mother was working furiously in the kitchen. When I settled into a chair in the den, my devoted and wise mother joined us. "I have cancer, Son" were Dad's ominous words. "Now, let's not cross that bridge until we have to," responded my mom. The doctor suspected the dread disease existed based on his reading of a chest x-ray. A biopsy was scheduled for Monday.

Monday found me in Ann Arbor, Michigan. No surprise. My parents had insisted that I go on this ten-day business trip, but by Monday night I was back home. The biopsy confirmed the worst— lung cancer. My dad had not smoked a cigarette in twenty-two years, but the thirty years prior to his wise decision to quit caught up with him. Worse yet, the cancer had spread beyond his lung. Surgery was not a viable option. Without radiation and chemotherapy, my father had thirty to sixty earthly days left. With treatment, eighteen months at best.

God Got My Attention

For several years I had walked the dangerous high wire of self-gratification. Now the inevitable happened: the imbalance of my life caused a free fall. An onslaught of words, mental images, and questions came at me so quickly that I felt like a race car driver who had lost control. Ultimately, I crashed. My high-speed life hit a wall.

God looked down on my pitiful state and drew me near. He said, "I am going to teach you something. Are you listening?" Luke records Jesus' parable about a man who stored up treasure to make his life easy. But Jesus warned, "Watch out! Be on your guard against all kinds of greed; a man's life does not consist in the abundance of his possessions" (Luke 12:15).

Jesus meant that a single-minded focus on building wealth is ungodly. Such a lifestyle is not properly balanced and, therefore, will not help us in our time of need. God told the man in the parable, "You fool! This very night your life will be demanded from you. Then who will get what you have prepared for yourself?" (Luke 12:20). In the final hour of our earthly walk, will any of the possessions we have amassed do us any good?

I had been building monetary wealth to the exclusion of heavenly riches, physical health, or relational value. Using the backdrop of my father's illness, God showed me the imbalance of my life and the pain it had caused. My joy and contentment were gone. My relationship with Teri was suffering because I had neglected her and our children. I was unable to cope with Dad's cancer. My relationship with my heavenly Father was distant, and my witness was greatly impaired.

No Witness

I had no interest in transforming my workplace for Christ. To find out if I was a Christian in those days you would have had to ask. I supported others' efforts to evangelize a lost world, but I was too busy to get directly involved. If I had attempted to speak to a coworker about the Lord, I would have been forced to explain certain inconsistencies in my life. Why was I not with my family more often? How often did I study the Bible? What about my prayer life? There was only one explanation for these inconsistencies: my life was not properly balanced.

My associates would not have seen Christ in my life because work was practically the only thing that mattered to me. Of course my family mattered to me, but the hours I allocated to work amounted to so many more than the hours I allocated to my family or God that the priority was obvious. If God was so low on my priority pole, then why should my coworker be interested?

Where are you in your walk with Christ? When do you study the Bible? When do you communicate with the Father? What about time with your family? Are you taking care of your body? How many hours are you spending at work relative to the other areas of your life? Do your coworkers know you are a Christian simply by observing your life? If they cannot see Christ in your life, your associates will never hear the message of Christ in your words. How will your colleagues see Christ in you? I believe the answer lies in the balance of your life.

Taking Hold of God's Balancing Beam

The high wire walker succeeds in his trek because each step is balanced. This risk taker sometimes uses a balancing beam to help. A balancing beam is constructed specifically to assist the walker. It is weighted on one end, then equally counterweighted on the other end. If the acrobat's balance shifts, the balancing beam brings him back into line with the wire. The balancing beam is precisely calibrated to balance a person on a microscopic wire.

God has a precise plan for this world, and its implementation requires properly calibrated precision instruments of the highest quality. You and I are His precision instruments.

A Barretta is an Italian-made firearm used by our military and law enforcement agencies. Manufacturing a Barretta requires precision. The firing pin must be calibrated to strike the shell in the exact spot to ignite the explosion that propels the bullet forward. The barrel must be calibrated to house the shell within a hair of its diameter. If the barrel is too tight the bullet may not escape. If the barrel is too loose the entire shell may eject throwing the bullet off course. All parts of the firearm are designed to function together, resulting in an accurate strike of the target.

God made us multidimensional. We have working parts that must function together if we are to reach our full potential. But unlike guns or artificial hip joints, our working parts must grow and develop. God sewed into each of us the dimensions of our beings, but we must initiate and properly calibrate the growth of our various dimensions to ensure their harmony.

Jesus: An Example of Balance

Luke reported that "Jesus grew in wisdom and stature, and in favor with God and men" (Luke 2:52). This verse is our only clue to the eighteen hidden years of Jesus' life between the ages of twelve and thirty. During these years He learned the trade of carpentry. He learned the geography of the region and the routes to various cities. He must have negotiated the agonizing adolescent years and honed His skill in communicating with others. He invested thousands of hours pouring over the Scriptures and praying to His Father. These years of preparation were vital to the outcome of His ministry, yet all we know for sure is that He "grew in wisdom and stature, and in favor with God and men."

Having been made in the image of God, you and I have the same four dimensions mentioned in Luke. Like the example of our Savior, the harmonious working of these dimensions is vital to the outcome of our ministry. Proper balance, the kind of balance God desires for our lives, means the four dimensions live in harmony. But how? The answer to finding Christlike balance is priority. The word *priority* was not used in its plural form until this century. So, from the beginning of time until essentially our generation, a person spoke of life's one and only priority. Today we try to work God into the many activities of our lives. We make God *one* of our many priorities, and we control the agenda. The result is a poorly calibrated life that is often frustrating and unfulfilling.

Do you want the contentment a balanced life brings? Then make God your priority, your *only* priority. Let every other decision, relationship, and activity flow from your only priority—God. God promises to balance your life (see Prov. 3:5–6).

Growing in Wisdom

Wisdom is the dimension of life encompassing our knowledge. Living in the information age, the opportunities to increase our knowledge seem endless. So for our present purposes I am limiting the discussion of wisdom to knowledge of the Scriptures and knowledge of our work.

Wisdom from God's Word

The Bible is God's revelation to you and me. From its inspired pages we can learn every aspect of His nature. We can apply its teaching to any situation we face. It stands to reason that if we intend to follow Christ, we must learn His Word. Knowledge of His Word leads to wisdom. Paul encouraged Timothy saying, "From infancy you have known the holy Scriptures, which are able to make you wise for salvation through faith in Christ Jesus" (2 Tim. 3:15).

Knowledge of the Scriptures is necessary if you intend to capture your workplace for the author of the Word. You will meet harsh resistance. Be ready as Christ was ready. Once, the Sadducces questioned Jesus with the intent of trapping Him. His reply was, "You are in error because you do not know the Scriptures or the power of God" (Matt. 22:29). Can you confidently offer a loving retort to a cynical coworker?

Paul offered sound advice that is appropriate for all of us when he told Timothy, "Do your best to present yourself to God as one approved, a workman who does not need to be ashamed and who correctly handles the word of truth" (2 Tim. 2:15). How well do you handle the Scriptures? Think about how many years you have been employed by your company or the number of years you have worked in your industry. Then think about what you have learned about your company or industry. Now, ask yourself how long you have been a Christian. How has you Bible knowledge grown? If you are like most of us, you can't explain why you have been a Christian longer than an employee yet you know your business better than you do God's business. If so, take this as a gentle prod to balance your knowledge.

❖ Establish a specific time and place to study God's Word.
❖ Invite a friend to study along with you. There are hundreds of Bible study guides available in bookstores. If you want to get started today and you cannot make it to the mall, then open your Bible to one of the Gospels and prayerfully read.
❖ Record in a journal the impression God makes as you read.
❖ Whatever method you prefer, start studying as soon as possible.

Wisdom from Work Experience

Keep in mind that the knowledge we acquire through our work is an important aspect of our wisdom dimension. Work was God's idea. After He created Adam and Eve, "God blessed them and said to them, 'Be fruitful and increase in number; fill the earth and subdue it. Rule over the fish of the sea and the birds of the air and over every living creature that moves on the ground'" (Gen. 1:28). Being fruitful, subduing the earth, and ruling require work. Manual labor and good management are necessary to build God's desired earthly civilization and heavenly kingdom.

In his letter to the Thessalonians Paul admonished idle believers to get off their duff and get into productive work: "For even when we were with you, we gave you this rule: 'If a man will not work, he shall not eat'" (2 Thess. 3:10). Maybe you are able-bodied but presently are not working or not working up to your ability. Listen to Paul and go to work. Perhaps you identify with my story of tilting life's scales in favor of work. If so, you are probably reading this at your office or on a flight to somewhere. I hope you will take encouragement from me to add God and your family to your list of assets and set a new priority accordingly.

Balance with regard to our work means we achieve and compete between the hours of eight and five but not at the expense of the other areas of our life. King Solomon was a man full of gusto. Whatever he attempted, he gave the task 110 percent effort. He tried everything imaginable to find peace and contentment, yet looking back over his life, Solomon wrote, "I hated all the things I had toiled for under the sun, because I must leave them to the one who comes after me. And who knows whether he will be a wise man or a fool? Yet he will have control over all the work into which I have poured my effort and skill under the sun" (Eccl. 2:18–20). With 20/20 hindsight Solomon realized his labor—without God in control—was virtually meaningless. In the last days of his life, I believe Solomon longed for balance, a harmony among his pursuits.

In a properly balanced life, work complements the other dimensions of stature and relationships with God and man. This correct calibration is so uncommon in our world that the mere presence of a balanced believer can convict an entire workplace. Knowledge is critical, but this dimension of our being must grow in harmony with our stature, our relationship with God, and our relationship with mankind.

Growing in Stature

For me, writing this chapter has been the equivalent of attending an encounter group. I already admitted that I created imbalance in my life by choosing work as my priority. That confession was easy to make since it revealed a past problem. Now we are beginning to get personal.

Balancing the life dimension of stature has been a challenge for me. If we were seated in the circle of an encounter group, you would see the sweat rolling down my slightly oversized face. My twitching and squirming would alert you to some unconfessed problem in my life. If you are one of the confrontational types you would call on me asking, "Uh, Bill, how are you doing in this area? It looks like you really need to unload!" You would be right! I need to unload about twenty pounds. OK, I am out of shape, and, yes, this has been a chronic problem for me. Boy, I feel so much better now.

Would you like to join my encounter group? Step on your scales and compare your weight to the desired weight for a person of your height and bone structure. If you are an average American, you, too, are overweight. Feel bad? Do you think others are looking at you because of your hefty condition?

Physical Conditioning

Maybe you are out of shape. Exercise may fall somewhere after cleaning the attic on your list of favorite things to do. Perhaps you carry your weight quite well and can hide your poor physical condition from your friends. If so, you are luckier than most people. But there is a problem. Looking good for your friends is not the point. Being fit, trim, and physically fit for our Father is our calling.

God's view of us should be of concern. The Holy Spirit dwells in our body. "Do you not know that your body is the temple of the Holy Spirit, who is in you, whom you have received from God? You are not your own; you were bought at a price. Therefore honor God with your body" (1 Cor. 6:19–20). Would you invite a friend to stay with you and not clean your house before she arrived? Most of us exhaust ourselves preparing the entire house for the arrival of a guest. When we invited Christ to reign over our life we also invited the Holy Spirit to reside in our body. Would we treat an earthly friend better than the God of our creation? Frankly, I am guilty! After asking my Maker to forgive my lack of hospitality, I am committing anew to get in shape. I commend you if your daily routine includes time for sprucing up the hall of the Holy Spirit. But if you are convicted along with me, then I challenge you to get going. Oh, we know the drill. Jogging, cycling, swimming, walking, sit-ups, push-ups, and chin-ups are some of the dreaded activities necessary to tune up our tired bodies. Pick your regimen and begin.

Rest

If you follow through on your commitment to exercise, then this second aspect of the dimension of stature should not present a significant challenge. Rest: taking the time to retreat from the demands of the day.

Rest is not universally appreciated or understood by the world. In some workplaces, persons attempting to add balance to their lives by taking a vacation, scheduling a day off, or simply working a reasonable number of hours are blacklisted. Everything from one's loyalty to the company to their work ethic is questioned. I have encountered this attitude in my career, and I have concluded that since I ultimately work for God, finding balance through a form of retreat is an important witness for my human detractors.

Fortune magazine featured an article on stamina in the workplace. The reporter interviewed chief executive officers of major corporations. As part of the story, *Fortune* estimated how many hours the CEOs worked each day. I am sure Herb Kelleher, CEO of Southwest Airlines, is proud that his ninety hours worked each week topped all the other CEOs in the survey. Tony O'Reilly of H. J. Heinz ran a close second with eighty hours spent weekly in the workplace. None of the CEOs worked less than sixty hours a week.[1]

I realize that there are periods when working the number of hours disclosed by the *Fortune* article is necessary. But I wonder how much time these guys spend with God and family. I believe their work habits send the wrong message to a needy work force.

I don't believe Jesus was a workaholic. After feeding the five thousand, He "withdrew by boat privately to a solitary place" (Matt. 14:13). After being tested by the Pharisees and Sadducees, "Jesus then left them and went away" (Matt. 16:4). After healing Simon's mother-in-law and many others, "Jesus went out to a solitary place" (Luke 4:42).

Retreat and respite are not sinister ideas dreamed up by a loafing work force. On the contrary, these stature builders are the creative design of God. When He willed the world into reality, He rested: "By the seventh day God had finished the work he had been doing; so on the seventh day he rested from all his work" (Gen. 2:2). The Lord instructed Moses on Mt. Sinai to give the land a period of rest: "Speak to the Israelites and say to them: 'When you enter the land I am going to give you, the land itself must observe a sabbath to the LORD'" (Lev. 25:1–2).

I believe God says to work hard (as we read earlier in the writings of Paul), but keep your perspective. Rest your body so you can "offer your bodies as living sacrifices, holy and pleasing to God—which is your spiritual worship. Do not conform any longer to the pattern of this world, but be transformed by the renewing of your mind" (Rom. 12:1–2). Do not give in to the unnecessary and unreasonable pressures of the workplace.

Are you giving your work 100 percent effort? Are you working enough hours to get your job accomplished in a manner honoring to our Lord? If not, then reflect on Paul's admonition that if you do not work then you will not eat. Plan to change your habit of shabby workmanship. If your efforts do measure up to the Lord's standard, then take time to retreat.

* ❖ Begin planning a vacation or a long weekend with your family.
* ❖ Develop a hobby such as hunting, fishing, sailing, or cycling.

Growing in stature means giving control of your body and its activity to God. Hard work, exercise, and rest are God's design. Growing in stature is impressive. Developing this dimension of our lives signals our coworkers that something or somebody other than work is important. Still, our physical dimension must grow in harmony with the other dimensions of wisdom, relationship with God, and relationship with mankind.

Growing in Favor with God

Loving God—The Christian's Priority

Our relationship with God is vertical; He is on top and we are on the bottom. This picture suggests a chain of command. He is first, and we are second. He is in charge, and we are to serve Him and follow His orders. This is not my theory; it is God's command. Jesus issued this command in response to a Pharisee's question: "Hearing that Jesus had silenced the Sadducees, the Pharisees got together. One of them, an expert in the law, tested him with this question: 'Teacher, which is the greatest commandment in the Law?' Jesus replied: '"Love the Lord your God with all your heart and with all your soul and with all your mind." This is the first and greatest commandment'" (Matt. 22:34–38).

We are told that loving God is the greatest commandment of all; therefore, it should be our priority. Balance requires that we hold close and dear and first our relationship with God. Jesus taught, "But seek first his kingdom and his righteousness" (Matt. 6:33). God calibrated our balance so that He is the priority in our lives. If that priority slips, so will we.

Misplaced Priority

My friend Jonathan is exceptionally gifted and unquestionably successful in his field. Over the years his success translated into a modest financial windfall that he wisely invested with the help of friends. Everyone who knows Jonathan fully expected him to move on in his industry to bigger and more influential institutions. Jonathan was on the fast track.

One day another friend called with a news flash: Jonathan was in trouble for making some unwarranted phone calls. It turned out that the calls had been recorded, and in his attempt to obtain the tapes he was arrested. I was shocked, disappointed, and confused. How could this be true? Jonathan was always so together, so balanced, so pastoral. Yes, Jonathan was a pastor!

I spoke with Jonathan after the episode was made public. His diagnosis of the cause of his woe was (and still is) bone-chilling. Jonathan told me that the person to whom he made the calls had harassed his family. But that was not the cause of error. Then he told me several other factors that were involved in the incident; but according to Jonathan, those factors were not the cause of his mistake either. Jonathan blamed his unacceptable behavior on one thing: he had shifted his priority from God to his earthly investments. "I got focused on my investments and stopped doing my daily devotional," he said. "Oh, I was preparing my sermons, and I believed everything I preached. But when my daily communion with God stopped, I was ripe for Satan's attack." These were the memorable and instructional words of a man who lost the balance of his walk with God.

Jonathan's story points out that our relationship with God is dynamic and interactive. If we neglect communing with Christ, our relationship will suffer. This is easily understood in our friendships.

Have you had a friend move to another city? I have, and our relationship is not as dynamic now because we cannot be together as much. It is a fact that relationships grow when they are nurtured. This is true with friendships, and it is true with God.

Where Is Your Priority?

Maybe you need to add perspective to God's command to love Him with all of your being. God's perspective requires you to begin with the end in mind. This is the perspective of the parable of the rich fool building a barn only to realize that his efforts were meaningless in the end. It is the perspective that transformed my foolish life from barn building to kingdom building. I know that loving God with all my being and making that heavenly relationship my priority was the key to finding greater balance.

Almost anyone can build wealth if that is their single-minded focus. The greater challenge is to properly calibrate our lives so that in all our ways we are pleasing Him who loved us enough to let us choose our ways. I agree with the old adage that says, "You cannot begin to live until you are ready to die." The godly perspective allows us to look over this temporal horizon to our next life and see what is really important in this short walk on earth. When you gain God's perspective, the only response is to seek Him first and love Him with all your being.

Are you growing in your relationship with God? You have already been challenged to get into the Scriptures. Before and after you study the Word, spend time with God in prayer. Jesus built a pattern into His life such that Luke recorded, "Jesus often withdrew to lonely places and prayed" (Luke 5:16). This gives us some hint as to the activity of a Jesus retreat. I believe it is wise counsel for you and me as well.

Christian Growth Takes Time and Effort

Do you have a special place where you meet God? It may be your den, your living room, or some other room in your house. I have a friend who makes a daily trip to a tree near her house where she spends time in prayer. Does your calendar reflect a daily visit with Christ? Maybe you have a standing tennis or golf game. Perhaps you meet a friend or your spouse for lunch at a certain time and place each week. Christ is due at least the same commitment if we are going to nurture a growing relationship with Him.

If you are interested in gaining God's perspective in your life, having God direct your decisions, increasing your strength and courage, and understanding your life's purpose, then consider the following suggestions:

- ❖ Pick a time and place for daily Bible study and prayer.
- ❖ Journal your time spent with God. Record His instructions, the answers to your prayers, and decisions you make that indicate your growth in Christ.
- ❖ Draw a picture of your mental image of God. After a few months of consistent prayer and study, draw another picture of your impression of God's face. I believe each time you draw His picture you will see greater detail because you will be growing more and more acquainted with Him. Be careful, however; your tendency will be to linger here in the glow of His presence.

God wants our time and our attention, but balance requires us to use our time with God wisely. We then must use our wisdom, physical energy, and godly perspective to influence others. God wants us to reach out to others, especially our coworkers.

Growing in Favor with Man

Our relationship with God flows up and down, top to bottom, bottom to top; however, our relationships with our fellow travelers are lateral, side to side, horizontal.

We are not islands unto ourselves. Many of us attempt to live the illusion that we are independent. Some say, "I have no need for others. I am perfectly happy by myself." It is true that at times all of us need time alone. But God designed us to be with others. Whether we admit it or not, God wove into us the need to have friends and the need to be a friend. We must get involved with others. God not only designed us to interact, He commanded it. After Jesus told the

Pharisees that the greatest command is loving God, He completed the directive saying, "The second is this: 'Love your neighbor as yourself'" (Mark 12:31).

Know Your "Neighbor"

Dr. James Dobson tells a story about a series of lectures he delivered at a seminary. On the first day of his lecture series, Dr. Dobson spoke on the issue of inferiority and related a story about Danny. Later in the day, Dobson returned to his room and found this anonymous note under the door: "I am one of the Dannys you spoke about today. For years I have suffered from the feeling of inferiority."

The next day Dr. Dobson discussed the note with the students. Eventually, the student who wrote the note identified himself. The administrators were surprised. They said he was the last person they imagined would wrestle with feelings of inferiority.

A few weeks after his return home, Dr. Dobson received a call from one of the students at the seminary. The young man reported that a seminary student had committed suicide. He had hanged himself in the basement of his apartment building. The caller went on to tell Dobson that the dead student was one of his four roommates. Full of remorse, the surviving student said that five days had passed before anyone missed him. Focused on their own pursuits, the seminarians discounted their friend's absence.[2]

Call up the mental pictures of your coworkers. Are you involved in their lives? Have you ever called them at home to check on them when they were out sick? Do you know enough about their lives to know their needs, hopes, and aspirations? If you are interested in finding balance in your own life, then flexing your involvement muscle is part of the drill. If you are intent on capturing your workplace for Christ, you must find balance and get involved.

Growing in your relationships with others helps you balance the other parts of your life because you focus on someone other than yourself. When you put others' needs ahead of your wants, you get your mind off your problems. You feel the joy of serving that brings perspective and balance to your life. You embark on a mission that requires time and energy. Authenticity is required. You must be real. Your investment of time and energy is often referred to as devotion.

My Father's Example

My mother and father were in the retail furniture business. Through the years they had owned several furniture stores, but their real business interest was in their Ethan Allen Gallery. One day my father received a call from an Ethan Allen executive: "We like the way you run your business, and we are interested in expanding in the Southeast. Would you be interested in opening a number of galleries?"

It was gratifying for my parents to be singled out in such a profitable way. Their years of toil had been recognized by the people at Ethan Allen. This gave my parents an opportunity to increase their financial worth. Naturally, my father responded affirmatively.

Ethan Allen disclosed the cities they thought were ripe for business. My dad traveled to each city, looking for land to build a store. While he was away searching out the best property, I, now in my teenage years, dreamed of the material benefit this larger business would afford our family.

However, my hopes of Jaguars and jets were dashed one evening at dinner. I asked my father how the search was coming for the new store sites. He responded, "Son, I want to talk with you about that. I know you are excited about the prospect of this thing, but I have been thinking about it. I believe it will be best if we call this off; one day you will understand."

He was right. In June 1988, I understood. That is when I found out my dad was terminally ill. I realized that he had seen his greatest opportunity in me, my brother, and my sister—not in his business. Oh, he continued to work hard in his business. But the more he had worked on that expansion plan, the more he realized the toll that bigger business would have taken on his family. He also realized that the increased investment of his time and energy would have detracted from his current employees, some of whom saw him as a father figure.

Paul admonished the Romans, "Be devoted to one another in brotherly love. Honor one another above yourselves" (Rom. 12:10). Devotion is risky because it causes you to invest your time and energy in another person with no guarantee that the person will appreciate your effort. The logical and easy decision for my dad would have been to pursue the wealth-building path of more stores.

But he bucked the urging of friends and invested in the people in his life—family and employees. My dad knew that no amount of success could ever overcome a single failure at home.

The world says to grow your business regardless of the circumstances at home. God's Word says you should be devoted to one another. My dad knew he could not remain devoted to his family and employees if he chose to grow the business. Maybe others can properly balance such a heavy load and, if so, then keep building. But remain devoted to one another.

Invest your time in your colleagues. The following are just a few suggestions of things you can do:

❖ Invite a coworker to eat lunch
❖ Offer to carpool
❖ Organize an office outing
❖ Invite a colleague to church
❖ Call them when they are sick
❖ Take a meal to them on joyful and sad occasions
❖ Offer books and other resources
❖ Mail them a birthday card and Christmas and Easter greetings.

This takes time, but that is the nature of devotion. You must invest your time and energy in another person if you are serious about finding balance in your life and transforming your workplace for Christ. Until people know you are truly devoted to them, they won't open their hearts to you and your message.

Growing in relation to man is vital to living a balanced life. But our earthly relationships must grow in harmony with the other dimensions of wisdom, stature, and our relationship to God.

Evidence of a Balanced Life

Nine months after my father was diagnosed with cancer he went home to be with the Lord. God used those nine months to begin a work in me that continues. God used the last days of my father's life to teach me about balance.

Most people consider death their most dreaded fear. Not my dad. I watched as he fought cancer. The disease was painful and debilitating, yet he spoke to me about the future—places he wanted to visit and things he wanted to accomplish ten years into the future. I would respond, "But dad . . .," and he would interrupt me with a statement attesting to the power and sovereignty of God.

Dad's life was in God's hands, properly calibrated and balanced. He enjoyed the evidences of a balanced life—contentment and joy. He felt that unique, peaceful satisfaction that only God can give. It was his contentment and joy in Christ that carried him through the dark days just prior to his death.

During those days I felt like a baby in an incubator, God's incubator. I was encased in the circumstance of my father's illness and death, and I was wrapped in the warm blanket of God's love. Looking back now, I see God's protection and teaching. Through my father I learned the need for balance. The Lord honored by baby-like steps toward finding harmony among my life's dimensions.

I have not yet set foot on the other end of my high wire. Finding balance is not a single event. Rather, it is a lifestyle that makes God our only priority. Nonetheless, God has allowed me to experience a eureka of contentment and joy as I follow Him down "Balanced Boulevard."

You will experience the peace and power of God's contentment and joy if you seek the balance He designed. Then, as you follow the leading of the Holy Spirit, something amazing will begin to occur. Capturing your workplace for Christ will become as natural as the change of seasons. Your colleagues will begin to ask, "What is different about you? You seem so at peace. What do you have that I do not?"

Your witness will become magnetic. Others will be drawn to you. Then all you will have to do is give your associates the answer—Jesus Christ.

The four dimensions of your life—wisdom, stature, spiritual, and social—are designed to be in harmony. Your chore is to make God your priority, allowing Him to calibrate your life. Thankfully, God has given you tangible evidence of a balanced life that is pleasing to Him—joy and contentment.

5

Accountability
Insurance for Obedience

Oliver Wendell Holmes, the great jurist, once said his most awesome thought was that one day he would stand in judgment before a Holy God. As an attorney and judge, Holmes knew well the finality of judgment. No doubt he had rendered life-altering judgments hundreds of times. Yet this seasoned legal veteran was awestruck by the thought of God rendering a final judgment on his life.

All of us face the same fate. One day we will stand before God and hear His judgment of our lives. On that day we will face the ultimate accounting, our most intensive audit. What will be His judgment of your life?

Imagine you are standing before God. Based on your life to date, what will He say? If I were there today, I can imagine God sitting on His throne reaching for my file. Behind Him, just inside the gates, I would see my grandmother, Teri's grandparents, my uncle, and some other relatives I have never met. Several friends would round out the crowd. Then right in front leading the cheer would stand my father. Knowing my dad, his cheers would be loud and continuous, and his Cheshire cat grin would be smeared across his face in anticipation of my entry. But God, being the just and fair judge that He is, would not consider their pleas. My life must speak for itself. He would read from my file, cleansed by the blood of Christ, and render His eternal decision.

How does your mental movie of your ultimate accounting make you feel? Are you peaceful and content with your life? Or are you remembering persons you should have shared Christ with but did not? Are you wondering what His decision will be, or are you confident of your destiny? If you are like me, you want to do everything you can in this life to ensure a heavenly "well done" from our devine Judge.

God's Audit

It is common in the workworld to set up programs that seek to ensure compliance with corporate directives. We call these programs "audits." Most employees dislike the audit process, but ironically, it is the audit that saves most of us from peril. Most audits are designed to reveal deficiencies early on so a problem can be corrected before it becomes catastrophic. Cash reconciliations, monitoring the number of days it takes to respond to a customer request, and counting defects resulting from a manufacturing process are common audit procedures.

Most of us employ an audit process in our personal affairs as well. Reconciling our bank statement on a monthly basis is an example of audit, and we are all painfully aware of the annual April 15 reconciliation of our tax payments. If we receive an annual review at our place of employment, then we know the power and benefit of an annual audit.

If audits are positive and helpful at work and at home, then why do most of us neglect the most powerful and helpful audit of all? Why do we neglect a spiritual audit? From the beginning of time man has needed an ongoing spiritual audit, a process of accountability. What if Adam and Eve had agreed to be accountable to one another for their thoughts and actions? What if Adam had responded to Eve's fruitful seduction with an objective observation regarding the deadly potential of such an indulgence? What if Cain had linked his life with another who probed his thoughts? Maybe his murderous mindset could have been changed.

Looking through a Worldly Lens

Human nature has not changed in the years since creation. We still resist accountability. Bausch and Lomb, the maker of eyeglasses, had a problem with accountability. For twelve straight years the company reported double-digit growth in sales and earnings. But in 1994, their fast-paced growth ended as revelations of hyped-up sales came to light. During the dozen preceding years, Chairman Daniel Gill focused his managers on the numbers, telling his managers to "make the numbers but don't do anything stupid."[1] His executives, however, responded to his message saying, "I'd be stupid not to make the numbers." Gill's goal of numbers at any cost caused some managers to cut corners and falsify sales, thereby increasing earnings. Where was the accountability? I suspect it was an ugly word at Bausch and Lomb during those twelve years. A solid process of accountability would have identified many of the company's problems early on, possibly forestalling its meltdown.

Bausch and Lomb is but one example of our need for workplace accountability. Unfortunately, there are thousands of other examples where accountability is missing. Yet in this values vacuum exists an unprecedented opportunity for followers of Jesus Christ.

Throughout my career I have been advised to learn to separate my spiritual life from my secular life. That is, leave God at church and show up at work devoid of any spiritual thoughts or actions. In the past I have responded, and I will continue to respond, that our goal as Christians is to integrate our spiritual dimension with the other areas of our lives. We are spiritual beings. Every decision we make flows from our understanding of, and our obedience to, God. If we choose to do our best at work, that is a God-honoring decision. If we choose to overeat at lunch, that is a poor spiritual decision. Too often, I am guilty of eating more than my fair share at lunch. Frankly, I need some accountability to ensure my obedience to God in this area. You probably have areas of your life that are somewhat out of control too. The helping hand of accountability may be your answer as well. Accountability is necessary if we are going to capture our workplaces for Christ.

Why Do We Need Workplace Accountability?

There are four basic reasons why we need to seek accountability in the workplace.

Satan Is Always at Work

Satan roams the landscape looking for our weak moments. We are his prey. "Be self-controlled and alert. Your enemy the devil prowls around like a roaring lion looking for someone to devour" (1 Pet. 5:8). Satan's appetite for luring Christians away from God cannot be satisfied. You and I wear invisible bull's-eyes seen only by Satan. We must become accountable to one another if we are to defeat the devil's cunning ways.

We Are Fallen Sinners

Paul said, "For all have sinned and fall short of the glory of God" (Rom. 3:23). A second need for accountability is our fallen nature, our propensity to sin. Adam, Eve, Cain, you, and I, we have all sinned. God gave us the grace to choose our direction, and we have lived shamefully sinful lives from the beginning. We need accountable relationships with each other if we are to overcome sin.

Others Are Watching

When you step out into the world and declare your faith, the skeptics begin to watch. For these would-be believers, we are a beacon of light. "You are the light of the world. A city on a hill cannot be hidden" (Matt. 5:14). One of my recurring nightmares is the thought that a person who is skeptical about God watches me and sees no difference in my life. These skeptics are at your place of employment; they are looking for compelling evidence of the Christlike difference. Loving accountability with another believer helps ensure a godly intensity to your light.

We Must Focus on Christ

"For we are God's workmanship, created in Christ Jesus to do good works, which God prepared in advance for us to do" (Eph. 2:10). Between Satan and our sinful nature there is a good possibility that we will miss the full measure of God's purpose for our lives.

Many Americans need to exercise in order to stay in shape and keep those unwanted pounds from accumulating. Yet many of us lack the discipline it takes to make regular trips to the gym for those hearty workouts. The solution: your very own personal trainer.

That's right; for a few hundred dollars a month, you can have the exclusive attention of a trainer who will hold you accountable to maintain your workout program. You may think this personal trainer craze is ridiculous, but it works.

Accountability in spiritual matters works as well. How can we hold off the enemy, resist our sinful nature, provide light to a needy workplace, and find God's will for our lives? Accountability with another believer is necessary to achieve obedience to God and capture our workplaces for Christ.

Five Steps toward Improved Obedience through Accountability

MassMutual is a giant insurance company. Periodically, this company commissions the "MassMutual American Family Values Survey." According to the survey, "A large majority of Americans apparently believe that values are declining all around them, while they remain strong in their own families."[2] In another survey, also commissioned by MassMutual, "seventy-five percent said they are living up to their commitments to spouses, children and employers. And ninety percent say others are welshing on their obligations. Eighty percent say they are able to meet their workplace commitments. Only thirty-five percent think their co-workers are equally committed."[3]

It appears that Americans believe "I'm OK, but you're not OK." But *we* are part of the society that *we* see declining. So, either Christians are not as OK as we want to believe, or an even more serious problem exists. Maybe Christians are not having an effect on the society around us.

Be honest. Is it possible that you have compromised your beliefs at home or at work? In your workworld, do you see problems and point your finger instead of extending your hand? If you are unsure of the answer to these difficult questions, ask yourself this: Do your coworkers come to you when they need help with a professional or personal problem? Do your colleagues comment about your faith or dedication to the Lord?

The time is now for Christians to accept our responsibility to God, other believers, and non-Christians. The time is now for Christians to become accountable to one another for the purpose of improving our obedience to Christ. The following steps are designed to help you establish accountability with one or more believers.

Step 1: Recognize the Lines of Accountability

Our nature resists accountability. We ask why we should open up intimately to another person. But understanding the potential of the relationships in our lives and making an intentional effort to build intimate accountability with another person results in improved obedience to God.

I believe our greatest accountability is to God, but supporting that eternal accountability is our earthly audit process. All of us maintain different levels of relationships. We all have persons *for whom* we are responsible. I call this line of accountability *top-down*. All of us have persons *to whom* we are responsible, and I call this line of accountability *bottom-up*. Finally, there are persons in our world with whom we are equals. This line of authority is *lateral*.

Top-Down Accountability. If you are a supervisor, manager, CEO, or owner, then this top-down line of accountability is easy to define. Too often, however, those of us in management resist the truth that we are truly accountable to those who "work for us." God through His servant Paul said we are accountable to our employees: "Masters, provide your slaves with what is right and fair, because you know that you also have a Master in heaven" (Col. 4:1).

I believe Paul neither condoned slavery nor agreed with the practice. Here he addressed the top-down relationship as it existed in the workplace of that day. Slavery as we know it ended many years ago in America, yet the top-down relationship still exists. The teaching in this verse leaps off the page to say to today's managers, "Manage counter to the culture." Paul was saying, "Managers, you have a responsibility to those you manage." Unfortunately, I have witnessed in many places of employment today an attitude that suggests, "Be glad you have a job. You could be on the bread line."

I too have exhibited this dishonorable attitude. There was a time when I was slow to return phone calls to people working under me. The message of my slow response was, "You are not important." Eventually, some of them approached me and shared their feelings. That meeting was one of the best in which I have participated. We established a regular meeting where those who report to me assess my performance. I became accountable to my employees, and my performance improved.

These interim earthly accountability sessions prepare me for the big accountability session with my eternal Boss. One day I will face God, and I will be held accountable for how I represented Christ in all areas of my life, including my worklife. That is why I established an accountability relationship with a young man who shares my faith in Christ.

Tank Tankersley is a godly young man with the courage to hold me accountable. He sees my work and the actions I take to move people closer to God. He levels with me about my performance, and he tells me if my actions and ethics are consistent with Christ. Tank is one of my earthly auditors, helping me grow in likeness to Christ.

Regardless of the number of people you manage, you are accountable. You need a partner to help you keep Christlike perspective.

- ❖ Take a moment to list the persons for whom you are responsible. If there is a strong believer in the bunch, begin praying that this Christian will support you in an accountability relationship.
- ❖ Take the people on your list to lunch and discuss the potential of the relationship and ask them to partner with you.

Bottom-Up Accountability. You may be the CEO or you may be the night shift auditor. In either position, you are responsible to someone. It may be the shareholders or your company's customers and suppliers. You may be responsible to a boss. All of us are responsible and accountable to another person for our work. Most of us acknowledge this line of bottom-up accountability.

Paul admonished the Colossians, "Slaves, obey your earthly masters in everything; and do it, not only when their eye is on you and to win their favor, but with sincerity of heart and reverence for the Lord" (Col. 3:22). Assess your performance against this verse. Does your work speed increase when the boss is near? If so, then you are probably not working as hard as you should when your boss is not around. You need to become more accountable to your boss.

Jeremy is a data entry specialist for a large bank, and he is dedicated to his work. One day, he realized that his effort increased when his boss came near his station. A certain amount of increase in the speed of your work is normal when you know the boss is looming nearby, but Jeremy felt his work habits were spiraling downward. Most people would have ignored the warning signs, but Jeremy is not most people. He asked his boss to monitor his work more closely.

Few people would have taken the course Jeremy chose, but such a strategy is smart and honoring to God. The boss did not forget Jeremy's uncommon request for more accountability. Soon he questioned Jeremy about what it was that made him so different! Jeremy's action served as a hook and opened the door for him to capture his workplace for Christ.

❖ When was the last time your boss reviewed your performance? If it has been more than twelve months, then request a performance review. Be prepared to discuss both your strong points and the areas in your work that need improvement.

❖ Ask your boss to monitor your improvement in those areas of concern.

❖ If your boss is a Christian, pray that he/she will be receptive to establishing an accountability relationship with you that would seek to improve your witness at work.

❖ If your boss is not a believer, pray that your witness will be bold and the Holy Spirit will prepare his/her heart.

Lateral Accountability. All of us have equals. This lateral line of accountability includes people at work as well as friends away from work. Both are important partners in the accountability process. Your lateral workmates are important because they understand the environment in which you work. Nonwork-related friends are important because they often bring a fresh perspective to your problems.

You need to establish a line of accountability with both groups. As I mentioned earlier, I had Tank Tankersley holding me accountable at work, but Tank also had me holding him accountable. Our relationship runs both ways. We meet periodically and discuss our workplace witness. We brainstorm, trying to find the most effective way to witness in our ever-changing workplace. We pray for each other and our coworkers.

I am also fortunate to have established an accountability relationship with several friends who are not affiliated with my workplace. We meet at 6:15 A.M. on Wednesday mornings. We have a marvelous time of sharing and prayer for each other, our families, and our work. Each of us has brought work-related concerns to the group for discussion and prayer. The objective review of a workplace problem is meaningful. We are living proof of Solomon's wisdom: "As iron sharpens iron, so one man sharpens another" (Prov. 27:17).

I am a better man because of my relationships with Mark Anderson, Steve Barrington, and Eddie Parker. They improve me. The weekly process of accountability keeps me focused on what really matters in life. These guys help keep my perspective godly, and I do the same for them.

- ❖ List your equals at work whom you know are believers. Begin praying that God will lead you to one or more of them to establish an accountability relationship.
- ❖ List friends outside your workworld. Pray that God will also lead you to His chosen accountability partner for you.
- ❖ Enlist both when you sense God's direction.

Step 2: Recognize Your Need to become Vulnerable

Touring the Coca-Cola Company's corporate headquarters in Atlanta is great fun. You see memorabilia from the earliest days of the company. A live soda jerk tends a vintage counter offering a wide variety of Coke products. My favorite part of the tour is the presentation of old Coke commercials. Remember the ad featuring a multinational group singing, "I'd like to teach the world to sing in perfect harmony"? The tour ends in a Coca-Cola gift shop where hundreds of Coke-related items are displayed for your purchasing pleasure.

You learn a lot about the Coca-Cola Company when you visit its headquarters, but there is one very important fact that is never disclosed, one piece of information absent from public view—the secret formula. Why doesn't Coke give you the secret formula? Because Coke is afraid you will tell Pepsi! You only learn those things Coca-Cola wants you to know.

We are like that too. We sit and talk for hours about our past successes and even some of our past failures. We love to show off our kitchen counters and cars. Home movies are especially fun to share with friends. We tell others what we want them to know. But when was the last time you shared your secret formula? When did you pour out the innermost facts that make you tick? Few of us have ever really achieved true vulnerability with a friend.

Hiding a secret formula is appropriate in the business world, but if you are serious about capturing your workplace for Christ, becoming vulnerable to another person in an accountable relationship is necessary. Once the recipe of your soul is distributed to a trusted few, real improvement from the accountability process can begin.

Becoming vulnerable to your accountability partner may take time. Trust and confidence in your partner is the key to vulnerability. Trust and confidence breed intimacy. The intimate moments with our accountability partners occur when we share the secrets of our soul. This sharing creates a baseline of understanding from which objective and loving accountability counsel blooms.

Yielding the core of your heart, soul, and mind to another also demonstrates your reliance on the Lord. The psalmist wrote, "I lie down and sleep; I wake again, because the Lord sustains me" (Ps. 3:5). David painted a beautiful picture of our vulnerability. When we lie down and sleep, particularly in the days of David, we are vulnerable to attack. But David said he could lie down and dream sweet dreams because, while vulnerable to man, God would sustain him.

God made us to be vulnerable. Paul emphasized our vulnerability saying, "Now the body is not made up of one part but of many" (1 Cor. 12:14). You are an individual part of a larger body. Paul went on to say, "If one part suffers, every part suffers with it; if one part is honored, every part rejoices with it" (1 Cor. 12:26). So, instead of doing the macho thing of denying or fighting your vulnerability, rejoice! You are not weak. You are vulnerable.

Ask yourself these questions:

- ❖ What is my greatest fear?
- ❖ What is my greatest success and my greatest failure?
- ❖ In order of importance, what are the three primary motivating factors of my life?
- ❖ In what ways am I like Christ?
- ❖ In what ways am I not like Christ?

Write these questions and your answers on a sheet of paper and place it in your Bible or some other safe place. When you identify your accountability partners, share these questions and answers with them. This will be a great first step toward the vulnerability necessary to improve obedience.

Step 3: Replace Tolerance with Loving Accountability

If you are a sensitive, loving person (reading this book indicates you probably are) then you may have a tendency to affirm your accountability partner and others even when they err. This point of accountability application may be hard for you. I understand, because confronting others is difficult for me.

Tolerance can be the opposite of accountability. Tolerance is a national epidemic. It is politically correct to tolerate another person's view or behavior regardless of its compatibility with the truth of God. No wonder we live in a confused world. Without accountability to God's Word, we sail the rough sea of life with no anchor or compass. Thus, any direction is correct if it is the direction you wish to go.

God's Word is the standard for living. If you tolerate a position or behavior that is inconsistent with God's Word, then you believe there is another standard for living equal to God's. If you are caught up in the tolerance movement, then you are putting the affirmation of man ahead of the truth of God. I believe God's first commandment settles this issue: "You shall have no other gods before me" (Exod. 20:3).

Holding others accountable to the truth of God's Word does not suggest you must be rude or hateful in your confrontation. To the contrary, Paul wrote, "Instead, speaking the truth in love, we will in all things grow up in him who is the Head, that is, Christ" (Eph. 4:15). We have the truth, and the truth does not need our heavy-handedness to have impact. The truth of God only needs our availability. Confront, but do so gently and with a loving spirit.

Mark's Discovery. Sharon worked for a mid-sized insurance company. Her boss, Mark, was a believer with a soft heart for others. He really liked Sharon and felt she had a great future with the company. However, Mark discovered, by accident, that she had embellished her expense account. Thinking the overstatement was an isolated incident, Mark chose to overlook it. In time, the magnitude of the problem grew until Mark believed the problem was so big that to confront Sharon would certainly mean her dismissal. Again, Mark chose to tolerate the problem. One day Sharon made headlines. Her problem culminated in her arrest on embezzlement charges.

Did Mark cause Sharon to embezzle? Certainly not! But he possibly could have prevented the theft if he had intervened early on instead of tolerating it. After her arrest Mark visited Sharon and attempted to share Christ with her. To his surprise, Sharon was not interested. She knew Mark was wise to her expense report trickery yet did nothing about it. In Sharon's view, if his God was not big enough to help her then, He certainly was not big enough to help her now. Employing loving confrontation early on—immediately—is the Christlike action to take.

Fred's Folly. Fred is a Christian and the CEO of a large company. All of his life Fred has suffered from anger and a bad temper. His employees would come to work each day wondering if this would be their day to receive one of Fred's famous screaming fits. Hal is also a believer and works for Fred. One day Fred explained to Hal that his yelling was scriptural. Because Jesus threw people out of the temple, Fred believed he was free to wreak havoc among his employees. Hal tolerated his boss's misguided view. One day, a coworker asked Hal about his faith, saying, "Why do you follow a religion that is so mean-spirited?" The coworker went on to explain that she had witnessed their boss, Fred, chew someone out, then, a few moments later, he was overheard talking about a program at his church. Hal got the message, and that night he researched Fred's favorite Scripture. Finding no reference to Jesus being angry, and after much prayer, Hal confronted his boss.

Hal's actions were scriptural. When Paul and Silas arrived at Berea, they visited a synagogue and taught the Scripture. The Bereans "received the message with great eagerness and examined the Scriptures every day to see if what Paul said was true" (Acts 17:11). Can you imagine holding Paul accountable? The Bereans did it, and the result was the conversion of many Jews. Your obedience to Scripture can have a similar impact. Become accountable.

❖ Pray that God will give you a new boldness as you grow toward greater accountability.

❖ Make a list of areas in your life where tolerance may have taken a foothold. Begin praying that God will help you replace tolerance with loving accountability.

❖ List the areas of your life that you believe accountability would help improve. List the questions you know would reveal deficiencies in these areas. Word the questions the way you would like for someone to ask them. Be prepared to give the list to your accountability partner.

❖ Have you attempted to hold someone accountable and found the words difficult to say in a loving and gentle manner? Maybe you were harsh. Take a moment to write an appropriate rebuke for that circumstance. Remember, the tone should be loving and gentle.

Follow the example of the Bereans and sift all teaching and behavior through the filter of Scripture. Lovingly and gently hold believers and non-believers accountable for their behavior that is not consistent with God's Word. If we are going to make a difference in our places of employment, we must affirm God's role as the most important person in our lives, holding ourselves and others accountable to the truth of His Word.

Step 4: Respond Appropriately

Imagine your accountability partner has just confronted you with loving correction about an area of your life. For instance, maybe you have been consistently late to work in the mornings and your partner takes you to lunch and gently mentions your witness has been impaired as a result. How will you respond?

The appropriate response would be to thank your friend and improve your work habits. Follow the example of David. David took Uriah's wife and had him killed. Nathan told David a story about a rich man who stole a lamb from a poor man to offer to a house guest. David became incensed by the story and asked Nathan to identify the lowlife. "You are the man!" responded Nathan (2 Sam. 12:7).

Did David get angry? No. He responded appropriately by acknowledging his sin and asking the Lord for forgiveness: "I have sinned against the LORD" was David's reply (2 Sam. 12:13).

I believe David responded appropriately because his attitude was godly. We know God considered David a man after His own heart. Maybe God loved David because of statements like "Let a righteous man strike me—it is a kindness; let him rebuke me—it is oil on my head. My head will not refuse it" (Ps. 141:5). We should learn from David and maintain a godly attitude, understanding that God uses us to intervene in others' lives. When a Christian friend holds you accountable for your actions, embrace the feedback and improve.

Heed Solomon's warning: "A man who remains stiff-necked after many rebukes will suddenly be destroyed—without remedy" (Prov. 29:1). A rebuke, no matter how gently and lovingly given, can be difficult to absorb. The world's response is often a punch in the nose or "shoot the messenger." But God wants us to be so intent on our relationship with Him that such instruction is received and taken to heart. To resist godly accountability is to hasten calamity. Learn from the example of David and the teaching of Solomon and respond appropriately. Embrace the message.

❖   Pray that God will give you the grace to accept the instruction and rebuke of godly friends as if it were God Himself speaking.

❖   Search your memory bank for a past encounter with a friend who was attempting to hold you accountable. If you responded inappropriately, then write an appropriate response. Remember, an appropriate response is thankful and purposes to improve.

Step 5: Get Started

Move toward a relationship that is based on accountability as quickly as you can. The rewards are great and the risks involved in waiting are high.

1. Consider the relationships you now enjoy. Evaluate those relationships against the lines of accountability that were discussed earlier (top-down, bottom-up, lateral). Choose persons who represent each of the lines of accountability and begin praying that these people will respond favorably to your request for a deeper relationship through accountability. Your partners must be believers in Jesus Christ.

2. Meet with your partners. The place needs to be located in an area where you can talk and pray together. That may be a public place such as a restaurant, or it may be a private place such as your home. Plan to meet when there is little demand on your time. At night after work or on the weekend may be a good time. I would discourage you from meeting an hour prior to the beginning of your workday or at lunch because the pressure to end your meeting will distract from your purpose for meeting. If no other time is available, go ahead and meet, but be aware that time pressure can become your enemy. Stay focused on your purpose.

3. Establish the ground rules. I suggest at least the following: (a) Agree that all conversations will remain strictly confidential. Do not discuss the conversations with your spouse, minister, or even your dog without your partner's permission. (b) Agree to be totally honest with each other, even if such honesty hurts. (c) Agree to be available for each other twenty-four hours a day. (You must also agree not to abuse this privilege.) (d) Agree to filter all discussions through God's Word undergirded with prayer.

4. Develop questions you will ask your partner. You may not need to ask these questions at every meeting; rather, you may wish to discuss these inquiries once a month. How often you use these questions is up to you and your partner. However, the mere presence of these questions helps us remember those very important points necessary to capture our workplaces for Christ. Listed below is a sampling of questions you could use:

❖ Have you looked lustfully at another person other than your spouse?
❖ If so, what steps have you taken to alter your schedule or routine to avoid unhealthy encounters in the future?
❖ Have you been totally honest and above reproach in your financial dealings?
❖ Have you been consistently on time for work?
❖ Are you giving 100 percent effort to your employer?
❖ Are you seeking balance between the four dimensions of your life: wisdom, stature, relation to God, and relation to man?
❖ Have you been intentional about your witness at work, home, and any other place you visit?
❖ Have you consistently spent time with your spouse and children?

Your questions should be designed to address the specific needs in your life. If the accountability relationship is appropriately structured, then Christlike behavior and thoughts will become the norm of your life. You will grow in obedience to Christ, and your behavior will show it.

The Payoff of Appropriate Accountability

One of the greatest joys of my life resides in the relationships I enjoy with Steve Barrington, Mark Anderson, and Eddie Parker. These lateral alliances were born out of our common church membership but deepened through our Wednesday morning accountability meetings. Frankly, the agenda for our meetings has ebbed and flowed. We flex according to our individual needs. When we need to share a specific trial, wise counsel is always found among these friends. In the years since we committed to our weekly routine, I have grown in my knowledge and understanding of Christ. My accountability relationships are a primary catalyst for this growth.

Interdependence

One of the great payoffs of accountability is the acknowledgment of our interdependence on each other. Paul illustrated this interdependence among believers in 1 Corinthians 12. He described the various parts of the human body and compared it to the body of Christ: "The eye cannot say to the hand, 'I don't need you!' And the head cannot say to the feet, 'I don't need you!'" (v. 21). What the eye can see, the hand can touch; and where the head may decide to go, the feet can carry it there. As parts of the body of Christ we are no less dependent.

This is the function of my accountability group. Eddie Parker may challenge my behavior or attitude. Mark Anderson will follow up, affirming and encouraging me to use a special God-given strength to change, and Steve Barrington will conclude by offering a workable solution to help me grow beyond the area of concern. Each of these men not only holds me accountable but by using their uniqueness to God, they flex their spiritual strength to hold me up!

Growth

The interdependence God designed into our lives causes us to grow and improve if we take advantage of it. Growth is the second payoff of accountability. Solomon knew the importance of accountability when he wrote, "As iron sharpens iron, so one man sharpens another" (Prov. 27:17). He implies the "sharpening" of each other is not only positive but desirable. We are to help each other grow in our relationship with God. Like members of a team, we should cheer each other on to score for Christ. This is the essence of accountability —growth in Him.

Many of us have labored over the question of God's will for our lives. Henry Blackaby suggests we learn God's will through our relationship with Him. That is, as we grow in our relationship with Christ, we will grow in our understanding of God's purpose for our lives. Thus, the accountability payoff of growth will actually benefit our work as we gain a better understanding of how the labor of our hands fits into God's will for our lives.

Obedience

It has been my experience that the more I know of God's will for my life the more obedient I become to Him. Obedience to God is my objective, and it is the third payoff of appropriate accountability. In Ephesians 4, Paul described the various God-given gifts of believers, suggesting obedience results from accountability: "Then we will no longer be infants, tossed back and forth by the waves, and blown here and there by every wind of teaching and by the cunning and craftiness of men in their deceitful scheming. Instead, speaking the truth in love, we will in all things grow up into him who is the Head, that is, Christ" (vv. 14–15).

Life is futile if we fail to live for Christ. "Speaking the truth in love" is Paul's description of accountability. He projects the payoff to be growth in our obedience to Christ.

One day you will stand before God and give an accounting of your obedience to Him. God's inquiry will not be limited to a few areas of your life with the balance excluded. On the contrary, God is interested in how you integrate your faith in all areas of your life including (and I believe especially) your work life. At that accounting your obedience will be on trial. What will be the verdict of your life?

Accountability is not a necessary cost of the Christian faith but rather an investment of your time to ensure obedience. Only God could orchestrate such a process, but the choice of becoming accountable to another is yours. What is your decision?

6

Excellence
Building Credibility for Christ

How does the McDonald's Corporation spell profit? N.I.X. When a family of five like mine hits the road on vacation you can be certain the drive-throughs at McDonald's and other fast food venues get business. One year we motored to the mountains of North Carolina and, along the way, we finally had our fill of burgers and fries. So, when we saw a roadside fruit and vegetable stand, we had to stop.

Doing Things the Christlike Way

My wife, Teri, and our oldest daughter, Lauren, hopped out of the car. Peering from the comfort of my seat, I noticed something different about this fruit stand. I had to get out and see what set this establishment apart.

The property was sparkling clean. Not only was the area immediately around the fruit and vegetables spotless, but the parking lot and roadside were clean as well. The space behind the fruit where the proprietor stood was swept clean. The display of goods was attractive, arranged to accentuate the natural colors and positioned for easy viewing from the road. The fruit and vegetables themselves appeared to be of superior quality—no bruises or scrapes. The owner offered only the best to his customers. He posted his price list in plain view and set the scales so the weight could be easily read by the customer. The proprietor himself was noteworthy. He was clean, smiling, and talkative. His demeanor was calm and peaceful.

The combination of inviting inventory, clean surroundings, and a peaceful proprietor drew me in. I remember thinking, *This is a very unusual place.* Curiosity got the best of me, and I engaged the man in conversation. I asked him where his fruit came from and how long he had been in this business. He answered my inquiries simply and politely. As we turned to leave, I told him that his stand was the finest I had ever shopped. It was then that I learned the difference between his stand and the dozens of other stands I had experienced. "I try to offer only the very best because I work for the Lord Jesus," stated the man unashamedly.

That was the difference. His product was excellent because he dedicated his work to the Lord.

What Is Excellent Work?

Excellence in your work is the quality of doing things the way Christ would do them. The natural outcome of striving for excellence in all you do is the building of credibility among your coworkers. From this platform of credibility you can deliver the eternal message of Christ.

Christ modeled this virtue when He, along with His mother, attended the wedding feast of a friend. Before the meal had ended, the wine was all gone. This was a disgrace for the host family, so Mary pulled Jesus into the kitchen area and asked Him to work a miracle (John 2:1–11).

This was Jesus' first miracle. His disciples were watching. Perhaps they were looking for some shred of evidence to justify their decision to abandon the only life they knew for a life following a Man they knew nothing about. Perhaps His act of turning water to wine came at a critical juncture in their relationship and helped confirm the correctness of their decision to follow Him. This work of the Savior built credibility among His followers.

This event also illustrates the commitment of Christ to excellence. The servants must have thought the instructions He gave them were crazy. Certainly they thought filling large jars with water as a substitute for wine was insane, but still they followed His orders. The result was wine—but not just any wine. This wine was the best, and it surprised the master of the banquet. "Everyone brings out the choice wine first and then the cheaper wine after the guests have had too much to drink; but you have saved the best till now" (John 2:10).

Perhaps you have not seen your work from God's point of view. If not, heed Mary's words to the servants: "Do whatever he tells you" (John 2:5). God may have put you in your place of employment to represent Him to just one lost soul, or maybe the potential for an eternal harvest is even greater. That is God's decision. Your decision and my decision is whether or not we will obey Him.

Maybe you do not believe your work is important enough to make a difference for Christ. Consider the proprietor of that fruit stand. Fruit stand ownership is not exactly on the list of most-sought-after jobs. Yet this faithful servant sees the potential to use his job as a platform for witnessing and makes a difference for his Savior through the credibility that results from excellent work.

If you are serious about transforming your workplace for Christ, then you must become committed to excellence in your work. The world of cynics and doubters is watching us. They want to believe Christ makes no difference in a life. Mediocre job performance is the standard in most workplaces. You can set yourself apart and build uncommon credibility by working the way Christ does—excellently.

The Essentials of Excellence

I enjoy following college sports. My alma mater is Auburn University. We have had our share of ups and downs in football and basketball. Over the years I have noticed a correlation between excellence on the field and a strict adherence to the fundamentals of the game. Auburn, like Nebraska, Oklahoma, Alabama, and all other great football teams, performs excellently when the team masters the fundamentals of blocking and tackling.

To build an effective witness for Christ at work, it is essential that you perform excellently in your job. Therefore you must master the fundamentals of preparation, perseverance, and seizing opportunity.

Preparation

Chip's Preparation. My brother Chip is a defense attorney and is regarded as one of the best in his area. He is highly sought after by civil defendants from across the country. Why? Because he rarely gets a bad result for his clients. His work is excellent. Why is his work excellent? Because Chip understands the fundamental of preparation.

Chip invests heavily in a competent staff of attorneys to assist his preparation effort. He spends hours and hours preparing every conceivable defense based on the facts of the case. He researches each aspect of the case, leaving no stone unturned. I remember a case where Chip represented the manufacturer of a pacemaker. He traveled all over the country visiting the company's manufacturing facilities. He spent days with the engineers who designed the product. In the end, Chip was almost as knowledgeable about the product as its designers. That preparation made the difference in the difficult case. Trial attorneys tell me they hate to face my brother in court because he is consistently the most prepared defense attorney. Chip has built credibility through preparation.

The Wise Virgins. Jesus taught the value of preparation when He told the parable of the ten virgins. He compared our readiness for His second coming to the preparation of the ten bridesmaids. In the parable, the ten virgins went out to usher in the groom. Five prepared by filling their lamps before they went out; the other five foolishly set out with no preparation. Eventually the groom arrived and the bridesmaids began to light their lamps. The five unprepared virgins asked to borrow oil from their wiser colleagues, but there was not enough to go around. The foolish five left to buy more oil for their lamps. However, by the time they returned with their lamps lit, the wedding had begun and they were shut out (Matt. 25:1–13).

You can apply the teaching of this parable by first understanding that you are the only one responsible for your obedience to God. You will be judged based on how you lived your life. The God-fearing lives of your parents or grandparents will not be considered on judgment day. You will not be able to borrow the preparation of someone else when the ultimate accounting of your life is taken.

Second, you do not know the hour of Christ's return. That point is made perfectly clear, but another point is clear: We do not know the hour when God will send a needful person into our sphere of opportunity. Therefore, we must always be prepared.

So, what are you doing today in preparation for the ultimate meeting with God? Specifically, are you preparing to perform your work excellently as a way of honoring God and building your credibility for Him?

The result of Chip's work not only builds credibility for his job, it also builds credibility for Christ. Chip teaches several Bible studies, and guess who attends? Yes, some of those attending are the trial lawyers he faces in court every day. Do you think these attorneys would participate with Chip if his work were not so excellent? Would they be interested in the driving force in his life if his work was shabby?

What action have you taken in the last month to better prepare yourself for your work? Have you attended a seminar or read a book relating to your industry? Have you taken the time to learn the scope and responsibility of another department within your institution? If not, take one of these steps in the next two weeks.

Do you have a regular time with God? If not, establish that time today.

What project are you working on today, right now, where you can improve your preparation? Do not let the sun go down on today before you have determined a way to improve your preparation for the project.

Perseverance

In our work we are sometimes confronted with circumstances that are unpleasant and unwanted. All of us have elements of our work that we dislike; that is part of the work equation. It is our response to those unwanted chores that may make the difference between good work and excellent work. Meetings are an aspect of my work that I dislike, especially meetings that continue for more than one hour. On many occasions meetings run longer than my desired time limit, but by investing a few more minutes, we often arrive at a solution to the problem at hand. By persevering beyond my personal time preference, we produce excellent results.

If you have experienced the stress of attempting to operate a business through a period of low to no profitability, then you understand perseverance. My parents operated a business that required large amounts of inventory. During the late 1970s and early 1980s that inventory was financed with the bank at an interest rate equal to 20 percent plus. The profitability of the business was so negatively affected that our family had to put off fixing our car, which had been damaged in an accident, because the insurance deductible was a whopping $250. The easy way out of those tough times would have been to seek protection from creditors by hiding behind the bankruptcy laws, but my parents were never the type to take the low road of mediocrity. They persevered and eventually produced a profitable business, which they later sold.

Cal Ripken Jr. Persevered. During the 1995 baseball season, Cal Ripken Jr. brought the principle of perseverance to life. In September of that season, Ripken surpassed Lou Gehrig's fifty-six-year-old record for most consecutive games played. Ripken's streak, which began in 1982, stood at an unbelievable 2,153 back-to-back games played by the end of the season.

In an article that appeared in *USA Weekend* Ripken said, "It's easy to do something day after day if you love what you're doing. Perseverance means doing it when it's not always easy."[1]

The road to his record-breaking accomplishment was not always easy for Cal Ripken. He related, "I was sick the week I broke Gehrig's record. I had a fever. At night the blankets were soaked with perspiration, and then I'd be shivering and then I'd be hot. I wasn't feeling very good. But I still went out and played to the best of my ability."[2] Did he ever! During that week Ripken hit three home runs and broke Lou Gehrig's record. What if he had given in to the fever? What if Ripken had not persevered? Yet he did, and we have a stellar living example of this essential element of excellence.

What is required if we are to persevere? Ripken says, "Perseverance is based on two components: effort and desire. You've got to really want something to get through the rough spots, and you have to be willing to put the effort in. I've had slumps. And for me a slump was a big deal because of the streak. People would say

I'd played too much, I needed rest, I was hurting the team. It was difficult, but I'd just work harder. If my hitting was off, I'd go to the batting cage and try to hone in on the problem. It was very calming to work hard and sweat hard and repeat the motions until hitting came naturally again. I had to dig in deep and work at it." [3]

Nehemiah Persevered. Ripken may have had an ancestor named Nehemiah. This man of God understood the call to persevere. He personified effort and desire and lived a life of perseverance. Nehemiah succeeded because he kept going when the going got tough.

Nehemiah lived a life of privilege and honor. As cupbearer to King Artaxerxes, he enjoyed the trappings of royal life. I imagine Nehemiah was quite happy—until he received word that the city of Jerusalem and the wall surrounding the city were in ruins. This broke Nehemiah's heart, and he wept and prayed that God would move in Artaxerxes' heart to give him permission to return to Jerusalem and lead an effort to rebuild the wall (Neh. 1:1–11).

Having been prompted by God, the king agreed to send Nehemiah to restore Jerusalem. Remember, Nehemiah had lived a comfortable life. He was accustomed to royal surroundings. The contrast between the king's court and the fallen walls of Jerusalem must have been devastating. Most of us would have made a U-turn at the city limits and headed back for the pampering of the palace. But Nehemiah was different. He was overwhelmed with desire to restore the capital of his homeland. He entered the city and surveyed the damaged walls. Immediately he called the residents to work. Starved for someone to lead them in the way of truth, the people went to work.

As their work progressed, however, opposition arose. First, Nehemiah encountered Sanballat and Tobiah. These naysayers ridiculed the effort to rebuild Jerusalem's wall because it would erode the power of their nearby cities. Nehemiah encountered opposition from those who would lose power, money, and prominence if he succeeded. Still, in the face of Sanballat's and Tobiah's threats of economic boycott, Nehemiah persevered.

Those two outsiders may have acted on their threat to cut Jerusalem off from the economic gravy train. That would explain the opposition Nehemiah encountered next from among his troops. Due to an economic crisis, some people had to mortgage their land. Others had to resort to the even more drastic action of selling their children into slavery. Shrewdly, Nehemiah approached the bankers of his day and challenged them to put the people back on their land and stop charging them interest. The bankers forgave the debt, the people went back to work, and Nehemiah persevered.

Further opposition arose, but Nehemiah persevered. After fifty-two days, Jerusalem had a new wall. When all those outside Jerusalem heard that the wall was complete, they were afraid because they knew the work had been done with the help of God (Neh. 6:16).

Paul Persevered. Paul encountered more than his share of opposition, yet he persevered. Speaking to the Philippians, Paul said, "Forgetting what is behind and straining toward what is ahead, I press on toward the goal to win the prize for which God has called me heavenward in Christ Jesus" (Phil. 3:13–14). Paul would not allow his past mistakes to haunt and paralyze him. When bad memories, like the stoning of Stephen, crept into his mind, Paul persevered. He "strained" ahead, not allowing the fear of the unknown or the certainty of imprisonment to deter him from his calling. Paul persevered and faced the future.

You Can Persevere. Maybe you are a CEO who has lost interest in your employees. Perhaps you are an employee who sees no connection between your work and the purpose God has for you. If so, you may find going to work in the morning about as easy as running in waist deep water. Once you are on the job, you may feel so tired that accomplishing a simple task is virtually impossible. If you identify with these or similar struggles, you may be treading on a testing ground. Your task is not to bathe yourself in self-pity, but rather to hurdle the obstacle with Christlike agility developed through perseverance.

How do you perform when times are tough? Have you persevered through deep waters? Excellence in your work depends on your perseverance. Consider the following:

Look at your attendance patterns during rough times. Were you on time? Did you stay on the job until the closing bell sounded? Did you go to work even when you really did not want to? A positive pattern of perseverance will be obvious. A poor pattern of perseverance will be just as obvious.

Look at your calendar during the tough days. Did you tend to break appointments and cancel meetings?

If your perseverance needs to be fueled, write down all the obstacles you can see to your work. For example, you find your work boring, you are having difficulty with a coworker that does not seem to be getting any better; you do not have the technology to be as effective as you would like to be; etc.

Next, write beside each obstacle your ideal desire for replacing the obstacle. For example, instead of boring work, you desire more creativity; your unfriendly coworker starts smiling and is pleasant; and to solve your technology woes, list the equipment necessary to bring you up to date.

A gulf remains between reality and the way you would like your workworld to be, yet you have defined that gulf because you know where you want to be. Take a simple action that will move you toward your ideal. For example, maybe you are the keeper of procedure manuals for your company. Typically, manuals are printed with black ink on white paper. Change the paper color. This is a simple move toward bringing more creativity to your work. Do not try to span the gulf between your current work environment and your ideal all at once. Take it in small steps, one day at a time. Persevere.

Opportunity

If you are reading this then you have opportunity. If you are breathing, you have opportunity. Opportunity to perform excellently in your work is both God-given and self-chosen. God gives us the ability, the talent to accomplish the task. It is then our choice to respond in a Christlike fashion.

You may wonder if God really called you to be the mailroom clerk or the supervisor of your department or even the CEO of your company. That certainly is a point of prayer for you—to discern the ultimate direction of your life. Nonetheless, we do know God has called us to impact lives for Him wherever we are and in every circumstance.

The real question is: "Are you willing to capture your workplace for Christ?" The opportunity is before you, and one evidence of your acceptance of the challenge shows in the quality of your work.

Jesus is the model of opportunity-taking for God. When His mother asked Him to replenish the wine at the wedding feast, Jesus could have declined. He could have rationalized that such action was not really necessary or that turning water to wine would not have a direct bearing on the salvation of those consuming it. Instead, Jesus saw the opportunity to reveal God to those around Him by miraculously transforming simple water to a flavorful drink. But He did not simply do His job. He took the opportunity presented by His job to do it to the best of His ability. Jesus produced the very best wine. His work product was excellent.

Paul advised the Colossians: "Whatever you do, work at it with all your heart, as working for the Lord, not for men, since you know that you will receive an inheritance from the Lord as reward. It is the Lord Christ you are serving" (Col. 3:23–24). Paul said to use "whatever" opportunity God gives you to reveal the excellence of the Lord. He did not limit his admonition to professional ministers. The calling is clear, and it includes you and me. After all, Paul concludes, we are not serving man but God.

Reflect on the quality of your work. Have you been satisfied producing a standard acceptable to man but not to God? If so, write ten specific actions you can take this week to improve your work.

Consider the opportunities presented by your work to capture your workplace for Christ. Make a list of those persons with whom you come in contact each day. In what ways can you influence their lives for Christ?

Do you have the opportunity to mentor someone at work? Maybe the person is younger than you or newer to the company. Look for those important opportunities to mentor another for Christ.

Pursuing Excellence

Excellence is a value the world understands. You may not be honored for showing love around the office. You may feel your encouragement is falling on deaf ears. Forgiving a coworker may even draw laughter. But perform your duties in an excellent manner and watch the response of those in your work orbit.

Excellence Increases Your Responsibility

Most of us want to grow in our work. We desire promotions and greater responsibility. Performing your work excellently often results in the recognition of hard work through promotions and salary increases. Yet sometimes employers fail to recognize the excellence of their employees; therefore, the company does not promote the people who are most deserving. That is why it is important to remember that we really work for God. He will credit our account appropriately.

Excellence Enhances Your Witness

"Make it your ambition to lead a quiet life, to mind your own business and to work with your hands, just as we told you, so that your daily life may win the respect of outsiders and so that you will not be dependent on anybody" (1 Thess. 4:11–12). Live a Christlike life and work in a Christlike fashion—excellently. People around you will notice. Coworkers will be astonished that the same person who is compassionate and loving, who always encourages and is ever ready to forgive, who leads a life marked by the balance God designed, and who is open to being accountable is also capable in the work setting.

Expressing the love, encouragement, and forgiveness of Christ will touch the hearts of unbelievers. Excellence in your work will open their minds. Then with hearts and minds attentive to the message of Christ, it can be presented with greater receptivity.

Christians in the workplace are watched by a cynical band of unbelievers. Many people believe you cannot follow the teachings of Christ and succeed in your work. We are called to prove them wrong. Work excellently. Work the way Christ does.

I have heard the old adage "If something is worth doing then it is worth doing right." In fact, I believe it is worth doing excellently!

Excellent work honors Christ and builds credibility for our witness. We must seize every opportunity by thoroughly preparing and persevering. Opportunity plus preparation plus perseverance equals excellent work. If we honor God with excellent work, He will bless us with greater responsibility and opportunities to share the message of Christ.

7

Communication
Created for Communication

When my son Will was five years old, we visited a friend who lived on a river near the Gulf Coast. The river's water was brackish, a mixture of salt and fresh water. Will and I spent hours fishing off the dock, catching several dozen red fish that we threw back. One fish, however, made the trip home with us and subsequently found its place on the wall of my office. This eight-pound monster was a variety known as a sheepshead. I had it mounted because of its toothy smile. The teeth look almost human. In fact, this particular fish even smiled. Furthermore, when the teeth were in full view, the fish looked like my grandmother!

Richard Haston is a friend of mine who operates Century Microfilm Services. Since Century microfilmed records for my company, I was in constant touch with Richard and his office staff. Naturally I wanted to share our catch with the Century crew, so I loaned the sheepshead to Richard. One day Will came home from kindergarten and asked if he could share the fish with his class. That afternoon Will and I motored over to Richard's office to retrieve Granny's look-alike. When we arrived, Ruby, Maxine, and the rest of the staff were in their breakroom eating lunch. "Will and I came to pick up our fish," I announced. The Centurions told me it was in a file cabinet in the next room. "Impossible," I responded, "the fish is too big!" Ruby said, "No, those cabinets are made for fiches, and they are there because I put them there myself yesterday." At this point I was really getting confused, but I knew where I had last seen the sheepshead, so I decided to look for it there. The moment I picked up the fish I realized that our communication was garbled. Static! I was talking about a fish, and they were talking about fiche— microfiche! After a good laugh, Will and I headed home.

Calling Card Confusion

On another occasion I asked my secretary to get a calling card for me. After a short while she informed me that the cards would have to be ordered since we were out of them, and she wanted to know how many to order. "Well, all I need is one," I said. She responded, "Maybe one is all you need for now, but you will certainly need more cards for future meetings." Scratching my head, I asked, "Why would I give these out at a meeting?" The fog lifted when she asked, "Are we talking about the business cards with your name, address, etc., on them?" After a good chuckle, I explained I wanted a calling card used to make long-distance calls!

Wasted words. Static. In the fish and card incidents I wasted both time and words. Fortunately these were "minor" communication breakdowns. Sometimes, however, communication breakdowns are not funny. Many times we fail to communicate, and the results are serious. Consider the consequences of failing to effectively communicate to senior management a potential risk to your company. What happens to your employee if you are less than clear about your expectations of him? What will become of your non-Christian coworker if you fail to clearly communicate your source of life and joy? What if after speaking with a colleague he or she is not sure if the spiritual foundation of your life is found in Christ or the New Age movement?

Since communication is so important to our relationships, work, and efforts to represent Christ, what must we do to convey and receive the intended messages?

The Requirements of Compelling Communication

Successful communication involves conveying ideas, information, opinions, and feelings in a manner that enables the hearer to truly understand the intent of the speaker. Thus, successful communication depends on both the speaker and the hearer.

I have lived through several terrible storms. Some of these storms ripped power lines down and left them lying "hot" in our front yard. Now disconnected, power to the homes in our neighborhood was gone. The source of the power, the generation station, was still working, but the medium that transferred the power was gone and so was the power to our house. For the power to be effective, the medium that carries or communicates the power—the lines—must connect.

The same is true with us. In order for the power of God's Word to energize and direct our lives, we must be in touch with God. Likewise, in order to send and receive the messages necessary for us to understand our work and the expectations of those we work with, we must be in touch with our coworkers. We must connect if we desire to communicate. Otherwise, we will be as ineffective as a downed power line.

Connecting to those around us requires style and a relevant message. Our message is *what* we communicate; our style is *how* we communicate. Both are essential to compelling communication. Furthermore, it is essential that our communication be compelling. Compelling is to communication what an electrical charge is to power. It is the zip that causes someone to remember and reflect on your words and then to follow through and act. When style and message converge, then communication becomes instantly compelling.

Your Style

Everybody has a style. It is a recognizable pattern you establish over a period of time. Picture a preacher you hear every Sunday. Instantly you recall his enunciation and voice inflection, whether he paces or stands still, his use of humor or catchy phrases. All of these actions define the preacher's style. Developing a style, honing it, and then delivering a sermon or a speech takes energy. Ask your pastor on Sunday evening how he feels. He is probably tired.

You also have a communication style that your coworkers know. Maybe you use slang or humor to make your point. Perhaps you are loud, dominating the conversation. Study your style as seen in your listening, voice, and words.

Your Listening Style

James offers this very wise counsel, "My dear brothers, take note of this: Everyone should be quick to listen, slow to speak" (1:19). When someone comes to talk with you, do you listen to them before speaking? If you do allow them to speak first, are you truly listening, or are you formulating your response while they are talking?

Solomon saw the wisdom in listening first when he wrote, "A fool finds no pleasure in understanding but delights in airing his own opinions" (Prov. 18:2). Listening first is a style of communication that seeks to understand the other person's point of view before voicing his/her own. Lending an ear accomplishes several important objectives. First, listening to another person acknowledges their worth. Second, understanding how to meet their specific need can only be accomplished if we listen intently. Third, the process of allowing the other person to air his or her issue often helps defuse difficult situations because most of us simply want our concerns to be heard. Additionally, upon hearing our own argument we sometimes realize there is room, and maybe a need, for us to moderate our position in business matters. Of course I am not suggesting we compromise on matters of integrity or faith.

Once your colleague has completely finished voicing his opinion or idea, begin your response by restating what you heard your friend say. By doing this you will eliminate any confusion about the other person's position. With that knowledge you can more effectively and efficiently articulate your position. You will be rewarded with quicker resolutions because you invested the time to listen. Also, people who have been given the opportunity to speak are more willing to listen.

Does your communication style include lending a listening ear? If not, try the following:

- ❖ Recall the details of a recent conversation between you and a coworker. Did you allow the other person to state his position or idea first?
- ❖ Make a list of your coworker's ideas or opinions that you learned during the conversation. Rewrite the conversation as if your colleague had been given the time to fully state

his position or idea in the beginning. Then rewrite your response with the full understanding of your friend's position. You should find that fewer words are needed to make more impact in less time.

Your Voice Style

I have worked under managers with diverse management styles. The worst managers tried to lead through fear and intimidation. I have witnessed the most mean-spirited chewing outs imaginable. I have seen the resulting trip to the bathroom by the recipient of the hateful attack, who would spend up to an hour trying to regain her composure. Having covered up her hurt cosmetically, the wounded returned to her place of service devastated and robbed of her right to be proud of her work.

Screaming and yelling have no place in relationships at work or anywhere else. Yet I have witnessed many Christians who are leaders in their church start out on Monday morning with a warlike mindset. These people go to work believing they have to be mean to get ahead. But to get ahead at what? As Christians, our objective in work is to perform our duties in an excellent manner with the demeanor of Christ. If we desire to get "ahead," then the "head" we should desire to get is that of Christ. We should put on the mind of Christ. If we are steered by His mind, then raising our voice should only rise to the level it takes to cause others to see Jesus in us.

Once a boss of mine was upset over a problem he perceived existed. With about 10 percent of the facts, he began screaming at me and instructed me to fire the person responsible for that area of the company. Instantly Solomon's God-given wisdom popped into my mind: "A gentle answer turns away wrath, but a harsh word stirs up anger" (Prov. 15:1). With the self-control that only Christ could have given me in that horrible moment, I responded gently. The louder he screamed, the softer I spoke. Soon I was whispering. Then an amazing thing happened—he stopped screaming in mid-sentence. I do not know if he lowered his decibels so he could hear me or if he was convicted by God to mute his tone. Anyway, he turned the volume down, and I was able to reason with him and give the other 90 percent of the story, which turned out to be positive for our company.

Manipulating his volume control was this man's management tactic. On another occasion, in an attempt to teach me what he considered proper management techniques, he told me, "Nothing would please me more than for your managers to call me crying because you had yelled at them. They will respect you more if you yell at them!" Wrong! Screaming only revealed his communication limitations and caused people to be repelled by his message. Our goal is just the opposite: we are to be compelling. Since it is estimated that 65 percent of a message is communicated through volume and tone of voice, this boss was rarely compelling.

Are you blaring your words so loudly that they are not heard? Do others wince when you speak?

❖ Pray that God will give you self-control as you encounter situations that have caused you to scream in the past.

❖ Memorize Proverbs 15:1, and meditate on this Scripture daily until a gentle response becomes your style.

❖ Anticipate work situations that are difficult for you by scripting your response so that an appropriate response will be ready when the unexpected encounter occurs.

Your Style with Words

We must keep our volume down so our words can be heard. I believe this is the most difficult area of our communication. The words we choose to convey the message of Christ or to communicate a new corporate policy or to introduce a new coworker are vital to the message being understood.

Paul challenged the Colossians: "Let your conversation be always full of grace, seasoned with salt, so that you may know how to answer everyone" (Col. 4:6). I believe "full of grace" means to allow the other person to speak first while you truly listen. Further, it suggests a Christlike, gentle tone about your speech.

Paul told his readers to season their speech with salt. Salt preserves and adds flavor. Paul, in all his writings, issued strong challenges. He flavored his messages with salty, bold words. We, too, must be creative and relevant and bold with our choice of words.

Follow the example of the Master of communication—Jesus Christ. Christ chose words that His listeners would uniquely understand. Consider His words to the church in Laodicea. Over the years the people of the Laodicean church compromised their faith and did those things that were pleasing to themselves. Thus they had become ineffective. In order for the Laodiceans to uniquely understand His message, Christ chose words that reflected their city. "You say, 'I am rich; I have acquired wealth and do not need a thing.' But you do not realize that you are wretched, pitiful, poor, blind and naked. I counsel you to buy from me gold refined in the fire, so you can become rich; and white clothes to wear, so you can cover your shameful nakedness; and salve to put on your eyes, so you can see" (Rev. 3:17–18). Christ described their problem by citing the very handicaps their city's products were known to cure. "Poor, blind and naked" describe the condition of a people known for their ownership of gold, production of an eye salve, and manufacture of white wool. Certainly this choice of words startled the Laodiceans more than if Christ had screamed at them, "You guys are not getting the job done for Me!" By using specific and direct words—local jargon—Christ dealt with their problem effectively.

Words communicate about 35 percent of our message. A gentle voice coupled with poor word selection probably will result in no communication, but the Christlike combination is powerful and compelling.

Once I had a coworker, I will call him John, who was my equal on the corporate ladder. Our company was being merged with another firm, and tensions were high because nobody knew whose job would stand when the merger was completed. John was known to be a hothead and a specialist in corporate politics.

As the merger neared completion, some of our employees reported that John was spreading lies about me. At first I chose not to believe the reports, but as the rumors grew I knew John needed to be confronted. I am not a confrontational person, so the thought of this encounter was most unpleasant. But above all, I wanted to handle this meeting with John in such a way that he might see Christ.

One day I took advantage of an opportunity to confront John. In a gentle way, I asked John if he had made some of the statements about me that had been attributed to him. To my surprise he admitted it and apologized, explaining that he had car payments, alimony to a former wife, a child in college, and a newborn child. "Frankly, I need the money and can't afford to be without a job, even if that means I get yours," explained John. I responded that I needed a job, too, but that God is in control, and if we both worked together, there would probably be jobs for both of us.

Could that encounter have burst into flames of fiery words? You bet! But the Christlike method not only produced a good result for John and me, it provided an opportunity to present Christ. Why? I listened to John's concerns first. Then in gentleness, I chose words that John not only could relate to but could be challenged by.

The following suggestions can help you improve your choice of words:

❖ Commit to learn one new word each day and attempt to use that word at least ten times during the day.

❖ Study the parables of Christ and list the ways He spoke in a specific and direct manner.

❖ Pull out the script you prepared as you read through the section of this chapter that related to voice. Now look at the words and reflect on the person to whom you are speaking. What words might you choose that are specific, direct, and uniquely understandable by that person? Now change your script to reflect those words.

You may have a problem involving a coworker. Until today, you may have sidestepped the issue, hoping it would go away. Now try to follow Christ's style of communication—specific, direct words spoken in a gentle, loving way after thorough review of the situation, which includes listening.

Your Message

Abraham Lincoln hated slavery. One day as he strolled through the slave trading marketplace, he spotted a beautiful young black girl on the trading block. Abe sensed the humiliation of the girl as the bidding started. Moved by her presence, Abe entered the bidding. Back and forth the bidding volleyed between Abe and another bidder. Eventually, Abe paid the highest price and bought the girl.

The girl had no knowledge of her new owner. Meeting Abe for the first time, the girl inquired, "What are you going to do with me?" Lincoln responded, "I am going to set you free!" "What do you mean?" she asked. "You are free to go," said Lincoln. "You mean I can say what I want to say, and go where I want to go, and wear what I want to wear?" the astonished young girl asked. "Yes, yes, yes," answered Abe. "Then I want to go with you," responded the thankful young lady.

Abe Lincoln spoke a life-changing message to this unprepared young girl. The message was relevant to her. It met one of her needs, the need for freedom. It was a message full of integrity, uncompromising and consistent with Christlike principles.

In response, did the girl run away immediately to enjoy her freedom? This young lady was smart. Anyone who loved and respected her enough to give her a message of truth and compassion deserved her respect in return. Following Abe was the natural response to his compelling message. Maybe she reasoned that there was much she could learn from such a man. Perhaps she felt safe in his presence. Whatever her motivation, Lincoln's message earned her respect, and she followed him.

Christians have an even greater message of freedom. Our message is not limited by time or circumstance. It is eternal. The message of Christ is relevant for any circumstance, any time, or any problem. A personal relationship with Christ will meet any need. As Christians, we know this, but are we communicating the message of Christ to those around us? The saving message of Christ is the most relevant word we can speak because it meets our need and challenges us to a higher standard.

Those are the basic elements of a relevant message—meeting a need and challenging people to grow. Whether the message is eternal or simply a way to improve a process at work, compelling communication requires the message to be relevant. If you attend a meeting about a problem your company is having with the conveyor belt on one of the manufacturing lines and you bring up a problem in the accounting system, your message is not relevant.

If you are interested in transforming your workplace for Christ, then focus on the spiritual and operational needs around you. Develop a message that not only meets the need but also requires growth. Then at the appropriate time, deliver the message in the style of Christ.

❖ First Peter 3:15 states, "But in your hearts set apart Christ as Lord. Always be prepared to give an answer to everyone who asks you to give the reason for the hope that you have. But do this with gentleness and respect." Commit to writing your testimony of how God has worked in your life.

❖ Verbally give your testimony to as many friends who are Christians as possible. Then make a list of lost persons who need to hear the relevant message of Christ, and begin praying for an opportunity to share your testimony with them. Be prepared; God will grant your desire to share your testimony.

❖ Be aware of operational needs around your workplace. When you identify a need that you can address, then script out your message in advance. Study the message to be sure you have addressed the most pressing need and that your message both meets the need and challenges you and your coworkers to grow. Ask for a meeting to deliver your message.

Compelling communication is a prerequisite for capturing your workplace for Christ. Our communication must be clear. It must be delivered in a style that reflects its Creator, and it must be relevant. If we invest the energy to accomplish this very difficult task of communicating, the consequences will be eternal.

Results of Compelling Communication

When Will and I attempted to retrieve our prize catch from Century Microfilm, we encountered a snag in communication. When I attempted to obtain a phone card, the lines of communication went down. When my boss screamed his message, our communication was blocked. But when Abe Lincoln communicated a relevant message to a needy girl using a Christlike style of communication, a channel opened up and the consequences were considerable.

Clear Understanding

The girl inquired about Abe's offer, and he responded with specific and direct words spoken in a Christlike style. The girl understood, and no expectation gap existed. She knew she was free to go because Abe had clearly communicated that fact. One of the great results of compelling communication is a clear understanding with no expectation gap.

Conversion

Did the young lady turn and run when Abe released her? No, she followed him! She made a conscious decision to go with Abe. You will find others converting their belief to yours if your communication is compelling. Whether the message is spiritual or operational, compelling communication will win others to your side or your belief, and in the process, you will grow in stature with God and man.

God uses His people to communicate His message. As a communicator for the Creator, you must be Christlike in your communication at all times. If the message is work related, you must be Christlike. If the message is eternal, you must be Christlike. When your style, words, and message are compatible with Christ, your communication will be compelling. Then God uses your compelling communication and produces eternal results.

8

Promise Keeping
Evidence of Your Anchoring

Sunday afternoon in most cities finds the retail trade bustling with activity. Shopping malls are open and full of people ready to spend their money. One of the biggest businesses in malls today is the fast food restaurant. In many locations food courts have been erected where the various food companies locate, and a large open area filled with tables and chairs awaits their customers.

Typically you find companies such as Taco Bell, Chick-Fil-A, Wendy's, Frank and Stein's, and a host of Japanese and Chinese outlets. One company stands alone in the food courts of America due to the promise its founder made years ago. When you visit any food court on a Sunday afternoon, you can purchase the wares of all the restaurants mentioned except one—Chick-Fil-A.

Truett Cathy's Promise

When Truett Cathy founded Chick-Fil-A he created a first-class restaurant chain without compromising his faith in Jesus Christ. Cathy is anchored to Christ, and he believes that God intends for His people to observe a day of rest and worship. For Truett Cathy, following God involves a promise, a promise to keep the Sabbath day holy. In the words of Mr. Cathy, "God blessed the seventh day and sanctified it, set it aside. The Book of Genesis describes the seventh day as a very, very special day. It is made for man, not man for it. I've accepted that as a principle and honored God by doing it."[1] In a world where it is profitable to open on Sunday, and in the face of a world that probably just would not get the point, Cathy is keeping his promise to God.

A Broken Promise

Chick-Fil-A stands in stark contrast to most of corporate America. I once attended a meeting of middle and senior management of a large corporation. It was the firm's annual management kickoff meeting. Company strategy for the next year was the topic. The tone of the meeting was upbeat, and it turned ecstatic when the leader of the company announced a new incentive plan for all levels of management. "If we achieve earnings per share above three dollars, then each of you will be paid a bonus based upon your salary. The higher the earnings per share, the bigger your bonus will be!" announced the CEO. Applause erupted, and the meeting ended as managers charged out of the room, eager to get back to their departments and make plans to ensure the earnings projection would be achieved.

Each department gave a monthly update on their progress toward the earnings goal. The managers made sure all employees were aware of the goals that had to be achieved and carefully monitored the progress. The teamwork among the management group produced unprecedented results. By October the company had made its earnings goal. They achieved in ten months what they thought might take twelve months to complete. The management team was excited. They had worked hard, and their promised bonus was assured—at least that is what they thought.

The chief financial officer sent a projection of earnings for the full twelve-month period, and it revealed an earnings per share of exactly three dollars. The managers asked the CFO how the earnings per share could be three dollars when the first projections they had seen only a week earlier indicated a much higher figure. To their astonishment, they were told the CEO had created reserves that had the effect of lowering earnings. Then the leadership team learned that the CEO had contrived the reserves to avoid paying the bonus. Just ten months after announcing the bonus program, the CEO broke his promise.

Promises come in all shapes and sizes. Some promises are spoken—like agreeing to complete a project by a certain deadline or to meet someone at a definite time. Other promises are unspoken. These covenants are implied in the activities of our lives. For instance, when you were hired by your employer, you probably did not specifically promise to be at work on time, but you made that unspoken promise when you accepted the position. Your employer probably did not spell out his promise to provide all necessary training and a conducive environment for you to succeed, but by offering you the position, they committed to that unspoken promise.

A Promise Challenged

Making promises is easy. Keeping promises is difficult. Circumstances change. Demands on your time may be different on the day your promise is to be kept than they were on the day your promise was made. You might even find it profitable to break your promise.

Truett Cathy knows the problem of promising. Closing your retail business on Sunday is noticed in our society. Cathy stands amazed by the number of people who mention his Sunday closing. The most common comment Mr. Cathy hears is, "Look at all the business you are losing." One such comment came to Cathy's attention through a letter he received from the developer of one of the largest shopping malls in the United States. Chick-Fil-A was a tenant in the mall, and the developer wrote trying to convince this promise keeper that opening on Sunday was acceptable, even to God. The writer of the letter even offered to contribute five thousand dollars to the church or charitable organization of Mr. Cathy's choice. How tempting! The mall is a safe place for people to go, and many of the Sunday shoppers are Christians, argued the developer. The mall's opening had become an "essential service" in the opinion of the developer. And anyway, the restaurant's employees' "Sunday workday does not start until after church," he continued.

Was Cathy swayed? Did he break? Truett Cathy did not even bend! The Chick-Fil-A chairman wrote the developer and explained his position, ending the letter saying, "Please understand, we cannot compromise on certain principles."[2]

Some people want us to break our promises. As the mall developer demonstrated, profit may be the motive. Still others are so selfish they will push another person to breach a covenant simply to get what they want. I received a call from my office manager in Texas. She was upset with one of her customers because he was demanding an exception to a corporate policy. She explained that the employees of the company were obligated to adhere to the policies, and a violation of the policy could cost someone her job. Callously he responded that he "did not care if it cost someone a job." Some people are so self-centered that they do not care if their demands cause you to break your promises to your employer or anyone else, including God.

One reason some people want Christians to break promises is to prove that Christ makes no difference in our lives. Christians who are serious about transforming their workplaces for Christ must get serious about keeping their promises. We cannot allow pushy people and our independent spirit to cause us to break our covenants.

My Dad Kept His Promise

Truett Cathy and my father had at least two things in common—their belief in Jesus Christ and their strong belief in reserving Sunday for rest and worship. During the early 1960s, my father was president of an organization known as Downtown Unlimited. This organization represented all of the merchants located in the downtown area. During that era all of the town's retail trade was conducted in the downtown area, which made Downtown Unlimited important.

In addition, our city maintained a law that prohibited businesses from opening on Sunday. This law was known as a blue law. A group of local citizens started a movement to repeal the blue law so businesses could open on Sunday. After prayer and reflection, my dad knew what he had to do—stand firm. My father and mother soon learned about the tension that can come from keeping a promise.

As the campaign to repeal the blue law heated up, my dad entered the debate. Initially the response was favorable, but the pro-Sunday forces relentlessly kept the pressure on city government to change the law. My dad applied equal energy to the opposing force.

The campaign turned ugly. We received mean-spirited anonymous phone calls. Some of my parents' friends turned sour. Some merchants, sensing the profit potential, turned greedy and turned against my dad. They put profit ahead of God.

Ultimately, the blue law was repealed—but not on my dad's watch! My parents sold their business in 1983, and I am proud to say they never once opened their business on Sunday.

Jonathan Kept His Promise

The godly act of promise keeping was evident in the life of David. Like all of us, he struggled with sin. David served Saul and became best friends with Saul's son, Jonathan. As evidence of their friendship, David and Jonathan entered into a covenant, a spoken promise of mutual loyalty.

Saul marveled at David's success in every endeavor. When the people seemed to favor David, however, Saul became jealous and plotted to have David killed. Saul himself tried to kill him, but David escaped. Then Saul dispatched a thousand troops, but David outwitted them as well. Saul exiled David to the Philistine front in hopes that the enemy would kill him, but David racked up victory after victory.

Ultimately, Saul instructed Jonathan to kill David. This was a crisis moment for Jonathan. On one side stood his father, the king, who controlled Jonathan's inheritance. On the other side stood David, Jonathan's friend, to whom he had made a promise of loyalty. Jonathan was a promise keeper too! He reasoned with his father, and Saul vowed not to put David to death. Then an evil spirit came over Saul, and he again attempted to end David's life himself, but again he failed. David fled.

Saul's war games against David continued, but Jonathan and David formed a strategy to discern Saul's intention. The plan called for Jonathan to alert David after he had again attempted to reason with Saul. Saul became so angry that he hurled a spear at his own son! So Jonathan went to David's hideout and informed him of Saul's resolve to have him killed. "Jonathan said to David, 'Go in peace, for we have a sworn friendship with each other in the name of the LORD, saying, "The LORD is witness between you and me, and between your descendants and my descendants forever.'" Then David left, and Jonathan went back to the town" (1 Sam. 20:42).

Scripture records one other meeting between them (1 Sam. 23:16–18). After that, David never saw Jonathan again. The promise David made to Jonathan remained hidden in his heart. Only Jonathan and David knew about their covenant. Maybe that is why he inquired of Saul's family after he became king: "David asked, 'Is there anyone still left of the house of Saul to whom I can show kindness for Jonathan's sake?'" (2 Sam. 9:1). In fact, Jonathan's son Mephibosheth, together with his family and servants, was still living. How did David respond? David gave Mephibosheth all of the land his grandfather Saul owned and even invited him to eat at the king's table on equal status with David's own sons.

Why would David go out of his way to keep a promise made in secret? David knew promise keeping was not a problem but an opportunity.

Three Rules for Promise Keeping

A pattern for promise keeping was evident in David's day, and the same pattern is evident today. There are three rules of godly promise keeping.

Rule 1: Promise Only That Which Is Consistent with God, His Word, and His Will.

Why did Jonathan side with his friend over his own father? Because David was acting in a godly manner and Saul was not. Would killing David have been consistent with God's Word or God's will? Certainly not. Saul's wish to see David die began in the evil desire of his heart. Furthermore, God had great plans for David's life that Jonathan may have sensed.

What about Truett Cathy's stand on the Sabbath business hours? Is his stand consistent with God's Word? I believe Cathy is perfectly in line with God's Word, and he appears to be following this first rule of promise keeping. What about you? Do you run your commitments through the filter of Scripture?

Rule 2: Promise Only That Which Is in the Best Interest of the Recipient.

Often we are asked to "help" people in ways that are not in their best interest. A clear example of this occurs when a transient person asks you for cash for food or travel or some other worthy-sounding purpose. I advocate helping homeless people, but the most appropriate way to help them may be to take them to a restaurant and buy their food for them or to accompany them to the bus station and purchase their ticket for them. Unfortunately, cash is often used for purposes that harm rather than help.

We must be shrewd because often we are asked to help people in the workplace when our involvement may actually hurt. Jake, my coworker, invited me to lunch to discuss a problem he was having. He sought my advice and help to stop drinking. Jake had been ticketed for driving under the influence, and his initial attempts to quit cold turkey proved difficult. I helped Jake find an Alcoholics Anonymous meeting. We met for lunch regularly, and I would ask Jake if he had taken a drink. For a while Jake seemed to make progress, but one day he admitted to taking a drink. Then a pattern developed. Every time I asked Jake if he had taken a drink, he quickly answered yes. I insisted he find a treatment facility and check in, but he ignored my advice. Therefore I stopped meeting him for lunch. Why? Because my continued presence at lunch communicated a message to Jake that his alcohol abuse was somewhat acceptable. My promise to share lunch and hold Jake accountable was becoming hurtful to him.

Sharon was Patti's coworker. Sharon was always late for work and asked Patti to cover her tardiness until she arrived. One day turned into two, then three, and soon a regular pattern had developed. Sharon always had a great excuse, but rarely did she have a good reason for being late to work. Patti soon realized that while covering for Sharon seemed compassionate at first, a destructive habit had formed. Patti confronted Sharon, ending the cover-up and forcing Sharon to confront her problem.

In relationships, the unspoken promise we make is that we will help each other grow. To keep our promise we must sometimes look beyond what we are asked to do and determine the real need. Being a promise keeper means acting on the need and not necessarily the request. My alcoholic friend *asked* me to meet with him and advise, but he *needed* to confront his problem. Sharon *asked* Patti to cover her tardiness for what sounded like very good reasons, but Sharon *needed* to change her bad habit. Patti and I could have continued to accommodate our friends, but true promise keeping means we act on a person's need, not their request.

Rule 3: Promise Only That Which You Know You Can Deliver.

Income is important. That is a major reason why we work. For some, it is the only reason they work. Barry is a stockbroker; he sells stocks and bonds. He works on commission. If Barry sells a security to a customer, he gets paid. If Barry fails to make a sale, he does not get paid. So who could blame him if he overstates the potential of an investment to make the sale? Many commissioned salespeople say whatever is necessary to get a sale. Then again, there are many commissioned salespeople who understand the long-term nature of good relationships. These promise keepers understand rule 3 of keeping promises.

Income is not the only motivation for promising more than we know we can deliver. Some people push us to promise delivery of a good or service that we know is not realistic. The easy response is to agree to something we know cannot be accomplished just to get the pushy customer off our back. Watch out! This trap will sink your ship.

Learn from Jonathan's example. He did not promise that David would not be killed. He promised David his loyalty and that he would signal David as to his father's resolve. Jonathan could deliver on those promises. Likewise, learn from Mr. Cathy. He can deliver on his Sunday closing policy. In fact, Chick-Fil-A negotiates this provision into all of its mall leases to ensure the promise is kept. Once an operator of a Chick-Fil-A store began opening on Sundays without informing the company. When confronted about his new store hours, the operator attempted to hide the facts. The operator was gone that day.[3] He had made a promise he could not deliver. Mr. Cathy kept his promise.

Take the threefold test. Are your commitments consistent with God, His Word, and His will? Do you covenant to do only that which is in the best interest of your coworkers, customers, and friends? Do you promise only what you know you can deliver? Tasks as simple and seemingly unimportant as returning phone calls on time can make or break your witness. Become intentional about keeping your promises!

❖ Make a list of any unspoken promises in your work life. Arriving at work on time, making productive use of all your time for the benefit of your employer, and using your employers' resources wisely are a few. There are dozens more.

❖ Beside each promise, post a grade you believe reflects your performance. Do not kid yourself. Do this after a period of soul searching and reflection. Very few will score a grade of A in most categories.

❖ Take a pad to work with you and record all of the promises (big and small) you make during the course of one week. Again, grade your performance. Then ask your coworkers who were the recipients of your promise keeping to grade your performance. Points of adjustment in your work routine will be obvious. Make the necessary changes.

❖ Brainstorm how to use your promise keeping to capture your workplace for Christ. Jot down your ideas as they surface.

Two Blessings of a Promise Kept

My mother and father kept their promise to God for decades. So has Truett Cathy. What can be said of you? Have you followed the example of David, Jonathan, Truett Cathy, and my parents? When others watch your life, do they see the consistency and firm commitment keeping desired by Christ? The stakes are high and the potential of a promise kept is eternal. If you follow through on your commitments, you will enjoy growing credibility as you become the person everyone goes to for results. Furthermore, there will be generations of blessings as a result of your faithful promise keeping.

Growing Credibility

Like most of the Christlike principles presented in this book, attaining the level of promise keeping that causes others to notice your commitment will naturally result in a growing credibility. Truett Cathy has been blessed with credibility by his Sunday closing policy. Certainly the Cathy family has benefited from the shared time of worship and rest on Sunday. But in his book, Cathy writes of another venue of growing credibility: "We find closing on Sunday attracts those people who give attention to spiritual growth and are family oriented. The fact that we have Sunday closing helps attract quality housewives and young people as employees."[4] Promise keeping not only produces the credibility that attracts potential employees, it also attracts potential Christians. This same credibility stood as the foundation of David and Jonathan's relationship, and it will serve you in your efforts to capture your workplace for Christ.

Generations of Blessings

My father and mother stood on their promise not to open their retail business on Sunday. They never broke that promise, even when their friends in the retail business waved their profit potential in their faces. I cannot adequately describe the blessing that has accrued to me because of their promise keeping. That blessing has little to do with the fact that they never opened their business on the Lord's day. Rather, my blessing comes largely from their commitment to Christ as evidenced by their strong stand for Him in the face of adversity. Solomon said, "The righteous man leads a blameless life; blessed are his children after him" (Prov. 20:7). I have been blessed with courage to stand for Christ by reflecting on their example. My parents' promise keeping is being used by God not only to bless my family but also to bless their former employees.

Chick-Fil-A is among the top stores in sales per square foot in virtually all of the malls where it is a tenant. They sell as much or more in six days as the others sell in seven. This confounds the developers and other tenants: but I believe Chick-Fil-A's promise-keeping style permeates all areas of the operation, and the customers appreciate their consistency. A blessing of their high financial performance is a program for young employees who want to attend college. For those young people Chick-Fil-A awards a one-thousand-dollar scholarship. More than five million dollars has been awarded over the years. That is promise keeping that blesses for generations.

How you follow through on your promises is the long-run test of your personal commitment. Keeping your promise is the Godlike way to live, yet it has become a novelty in many workplaces today. Spoken and unspoken promises are made daily, and the extent to which you follow through on those covenants may be the most visible difference between your faith and an unbelieving work force.

Knowing the godly process of promise making is the starting place for successful promise keeping. Properly anchored to Christ, you can make a difference for Him in your place of employment by making it a priority to keep your promises.

9

Stewardship
Acknowledging Christ's Lordship

Structures, Inc. What visions does that name conjure up? You might think of a company that designs and builds bridges. Perhaps because you know that some outdoor signs are called structures, you assume this company owns and operates outdoor advertising.

Not so. Structures, Inc., is now defunct. I should know, because I founded the business, and it taught me one of the greatest and most expensive lessons of my life. The lesson I learned was stewardship, and my instructor was the Lord God Almighty.

An Unstructured Stewardship

You may recall my mention of a time when my life was out of balance. During my mid-twenties to early thirties I tipped the scales toward the material side of life. My goal was to amass a net worth well over $10 million. That may sound out of reach, but I was on that road, and Structures, Inc., was part of my plan.

Structures was a company that offered structured settlement services to people who had received large settlements or judgments in civil legal actions. In our day of huge punitive damage awards, many people who have never handled large sums of money have received millions of dollars overnight. Our company worked with the plaintiff and the defendant before the funds were transferred to make sure the money was securely invested. The result of our activity was a lifetime income for the plaintiff and his or her family. A plaintiff who had little or no experience investing money received his settlement structured into smaller increments, paid with interest, over a period of years.

A structured settlement is a winning concept for everyone involved. I had seen several people on the West Coast become wildly successful in this business. I reasoned, "If they can do it, then I can do it." I was already successful in the investment banking business. Though I was consumed by my career in investment banking, I saw the opportunity to make even more money. Structured settlements looked so easy, and it took very little money to get into the business. With little investigation, I set up Structures, Inc., as a side business. After several months and thousands of dollars spent in advertising, Structures had generated a whopping four hundred dollars in income. Looking back over this business failure, I realized the venture was doomed before it began because of my poor stewardship.

Christ-Structured Stewardship

Jesus taught a valuable lesson on stewardship in His parable of the talents (Matt. 25:14–30). A man called three of his servants together and entrusted his property to them while he journeyed. To one servant the man gave five talents of money; to the second servant he gave two talents; and to the third servant he gave one talent.

When the man returned from his trip, he called the servants to bring his property. The servant with the five talents had invested the money wisely and returned ten talents to his master. The servant given two talents returned four talents. Then came the servant entrusted with one talent. He was not the risk taker his master desired. From fear of losing his talent, this servant buried it in the ground. Therefore, on the day of accounting, the servant brought back only the talent he was given originally. In response the master took the talent away from the servant and dismissed him into darkness.

Jesus used the imagery of the talent, which was a unit of currency in that day, but I believe His teaching is broader than simply the wise stewardship of money. I believe Christ used the easily understood talent as a symbol of our God-given opportunities. Christ was speaking holistically, and His message was, "Use it or lose it." God gives us ability and opportunity. He provides the resources and the relationships necessary to know and do His will. Our task is to use wise stewardship and invest our abilities, opportunities, resources, and relationships wisely so that God can achieve through us what He desires.

I responded to God's blessing in my life by unwisely using the resources, abilities, opportunities, and relationships He had given me. Like the unfaithful servant, I buried those God-given assets in an infertile field. Dirt did not cause the talents of money to grow in the parable any more than Structures caused my God-given properties to grow. Why? Because I had struck off in my own wisdom to pursue my own agenda. As a result, I believe, God withdrew His blessing from my endeavors. Let me be clear about this point: I do not believe God caused me to lose money on the Structures venture any more than I believe God rewards us with money for good deeds. But when God withdraws His blessing, chaos results, and success in terms humans understand is difficult to achieve. When Structures became part of my life, joy and peace left. My investment banking work began to suffer. My time was split between the two endeavors, and the problem child I called Structures began to consume more and more of my time. I failed with Structures because I failed to look to my Master for guidance in the way He would have me invest all He had given me.

Fortunately, God is in the business of redeeming bad situations and bad hearts. He used the Structures debacle in my life to teach me a modern-day version of the parable of the talents. I learned that a good steward understands and accepts his role of service to his master. The good steward acknowledges the authority of the master and sees his own life and all that is given as a gift from the master. Not only does the good steward follow the explicit directions of the master, he is called to learn the very mind of the master. The good steward knows his master so well that creatively and energetically he uses the synergy of master-given time, talent, resources, and relationships for the good of the master.

We have an Owner. He is God Almighty, and He owns everything. Time was His before it was. The talent or ability we think is ours is simply on loan from Him until our day of accounting comes. The money you think you made belongs to our Master, and the relationships in our lives are the result of His divine scheduling.

Stewardship in Action

The word *stewardship* calls up visions of budget campaigns. A steward is someone employed to manage another's property in the best interest of the owner. The good steward achieves the highest and best use of the resources given him by the owner.

In those corporate environments that are bold enough to use the term *stewardship*, it usually means expense control. This shallow mindset is, in itself, poor stewardship because we have a much greater opportunity to grow in Christ through the stewardship of our time, resources, abilities, and relationships. Missing even one of these opportunities is poor stewardship. It is important then to consider our stewardship in each of these areas.

Stewardship of Time

Time is eternity broken down into tiny increments that we can comprehend. One minute is the next sixty seconds of eternity. One hour is the next 3,600 seconds of eternity. God is eternal, and we are His eternal creation. Time is our best effort to quantify that incalculable gift of eternity from our Master.

During the Structures era of my life I failed to acknowledge God's ownership of what we call time. I lowered my sight from the Savior to myself. When I took my eye off the Eternal One, time became my enemy. Suddenly I had to have every material possession I desired, which required money, which required a profitable side venture. The result was Structures.

My time was limited; I knew that one day I would die. If I were going to achieve my goals, then I had to get busy. I was playing beat-the-clock, but I was fooled. During my teenage years I played basketball. One of the great tricks we played on opposing teams involved time; we fooled the other team into playing beat-the-clock. The official clock on the scoreboard may have showed fifty-eight seconds, which can be a long time in a basketball game. But when our opponent had the ball on their offensive end of the court, our cheering section started counting 10—9—8—7—6, etc. Often the guys on the other team were duped by the false countdown. In a mad rush, our opponent hurled a shot from the end zone in a last-ditch effort to score before time ran out, but time did not run out. In fact, we usually rebounded with time to travel the length of the court and score.

Satan uses similar tactics. He finds our weak spot, then plants the seed of a finite life in our minds. If it takes root, we may find ourselves with the same worldly attitude that focuses on the here and now instead of the eternal ever after.

Satan wants us to believe that time is ours and that we'd better go for the gusto before it is too late to build that net worth or sail around the world or whatever it is that hinders our relationship with God. But God says time is His, and we had better "be dressed ready for service and keep [our] lamps burning" (Luke 12:35). God wants us to use our portion of eternity spent on this training ground we call earth to get in shape for the balance of eternity in His presence.

Step 1: Acknowledge that the most important relationship in your life is with Christ. To be good stewards of our eternal clock, we must keep the priorities of our Master. To know those priorities as they evolve, we must spend time with God in prayer and Bible study. Using our time to commune with God and learn His ways is good stewardship. The first step toward hearing "Well done good and faithful servant" is a dedicated time to visit with the Master.

Step 2: Let God teach you how to measure every situation by eternity. Block out the roar of the worldly crowd encouraging you to play beat-the-clock with your life. Don't listen to the false countdown. Keep your eyes and ears fixed on Christ. The godly perspective of eternity will produce righteous choices that will please the Master. You must make big decisions, such as what career course you take in an environment where God can work you. I listened to the crowd who told me to hurry up, and that counsel failed. God told me to wise up and go at His pace.

Step 3: Use every circumstance to build the kingdom of God. Ask yourself, "How can I use every circumstance to build the kingdom of God?" For example, how can I use coaching my child's little league team for the glory of God? How can I use the time spent traveling in my car on business to glorify Him? And certainly how can I use my work to build the kingdom of God?

Use lunch breaks and the time before and after work for Christ. You are God-designed for His service. As a good steward, you should use your God-given increments of eternity for the benefit of the Master.

Start a journal with the following headings across the top of the page: Date, Activity, and Time Elapsed. For a period of two weeks, record your activities and the time you spent on them. I suggest you keep this journal at home.

Start a second journal at work bearing the same headings but add a column to explain the method of communication when the activity includes persons other than yourself. For example, you may record fifteen minutes spent on the Smith project. That entire time may have been spent on a phone call or in a meeting or on-line at your computer. Record the medium used.

Within two weeks you will discover areas of poor stewardship. You will see an improvement in your journal as you make changes.

Some areas of poor stewardship may not become apparent until your journal is complete. When the two weeks are over, analyze your results. Ask yourself these questions after you have calculated the percentage of time each activity consumes: How much time do I spend with God? Is my time with God uninterrupted and serene? How much time do I spend with my family? Is it quality as well as quantity time? How much time do I spend at work? Do I give my employer or employees all of my worktime? How much time do I spend at play? Am I building God's temple with my playtime? How much time do I spend at church? Am I spending so little time there that even the pastor does not know me, or am I spending so much time taking on jobs within the church that other people who need an area of service are shut out?

What does your allocation of time suggest about your priorities? Are you using your time to capture not only your workplace but your world for Christ? Reflect on your findings in light of the following Scriptures: "Why, you do not even know what will happen tomorrow. What is your life? You are a mist that appears for a little while and then vanishes" (James 4:14). "No one can serve two masters. Either he will hate the one and love the other, or he will be devoted to the one and despise the other. You cannot serve both God and Money" (Matt. 6:24).

Stewardship of Abilities

Maybe you are a brilliant surgeon or an acclaimed athlete. Perhaps you are a great communicator or skilled craftsman. Is it possible that you started with no ability or interest in your area of expertise? Do you really believe your success is due simply to your hard work? On the contrary, God weaves our natural giftedness into our lives, and He expects us to be good stewards of that ability.

"Then Moses said to the Israelites, 'See, the LORD has chosen Bezalel son of Uri, the son of Hur, of the tribe of Judah, and he has filled him with the Spirit of God, with skill, ability and knowledge in all kinds of crafts—to make artistic designs for work in gold, silver and bronze, to cut and set stones, to work in wood and to engage in all kinds of artistic craftsmanship. And he has given both him and Oholiab son of Ahisamach, of the tribe of Dan, the ability to teach others'" (Exod. 35:30–34). God told the Israelites to build a temple. He gave the people specific instructions regarding the building materials, dimensions, and layout of the tabernacle. Then God gave specific skill to two Israelites with the intent that they lead the effort. Notice how specific God was in His gift of skill to Bezalel and Oholiab. They had the ability to cut stones, make artistic designs, and teach others.

God not only gifted these two leaders, He blessed all the people with skill. "'He has filled them with skill to do all kinds of work as craftsmen, designers, embroiderers in blue, purple and scarlet yarn and fine linen, and weavers—all of them master craftsmen and designers'" (Exod. 35:35). To all the people, God gave individual and unique skills to fulfill His purpose.

Paul, addressing the subject of spiritual gifts, wrote, "There are different kinds of working, but the same God works all of them in *all* men" (1 Cor. 12:6). In this instance Paul speaks of our God-given spiritual giftedness and states that when God bestows different gifts, He misses no one. All of us are gifted with unique spiritual abilities. It is reasonable to believe that a God who gives every person a special spiritual gift enables every person with a special practical ability that can be used for His glory. After all, Jesus said in the Sermon on the Mount that a provision has been made even for the birds. The birds have the ability to fly and with their narrow beaks pluck worms from the ground. We also have the example of the building of the tabernacle as direct evidence that God gives special talent to all of us. God gives abilities, but it is up to us to be good stewards of them.

Step 1: Disown your abilities. Ask my friends about me, and they will likely tell you I am a people person. I tell you this because I have learned that my ability to relate to people began when God sewed that skill into my being.

Taking credit for a God-given talent is a very human thing to do. I could say that over the years I developed the ability to interact effectively with others. That self-centered approach would lead you to believe that through my own hard work I trained and developed the skill. That attitude would also disclose my poor stewardship in the area of God-given abilities. My Master made every part of me. "My frame was not hidden from you when I was made" (Ps. 139:15).

Have you ever taken credit for an idea that originated with your coworker? If so, you know the difficulty of developing and implementing the idea on your own. The same is true with your God-given abilities. Disown your abilities. Acknowledge God as the Creator.

Step 2: Accept your responsibility to develop your God-given gift. "Then Moses summoned Bezalel and Oholiab and every skilled person to whom the LORD had given ability and who was willing to come and do the work" (Exod. 36:2). Speaking of the people, Moses refered to those who were "willing to come and do the work." Thus, there must have been some people who were unwilling to develop and use their abilities for the One who created the abilities in them. We are not robots directed by God through His hand-held remote control. We are created in His image and specially gifted with abilities which glorify Him, when deployed for the benefit of our Master. We should be compelled to actions that maximize our God-given ability out of respect and love for the One that made us. To do so, we must first acknowledge the Master's creative hand in our lives; then it is up to us to pursue God by developing that ability He sewed into each of us.

How are you developing your God-given ability? Honing your skill is good stewardship of the ability the Master has given you. From woodworking to brain surgery, there are resources and conferences that spur the development of your ability. Go and grow.

Step 3: Use your talents to build God's kingdom. "So Bezalel, Oholiab and every skilled person to whom the LORD has given skill and ability to know how to carry out all the work of constructing the sanctuary are to do the work just as the LORD has commanded" (Exod. 36:1). Moses added the admonition that all the people were to use their God-given skill just as the Lord had commanded.

Perhaps you are a physician who does not feel called to the foreign mission field. So, how can you use your Master-made talent for Him? Two of my close friends are physicians. Steve Barrington is an orthopedic surgeon, and Mark Anderson is a gastroenterologist. Neither Steve nor Mark are called to vocational mission work, yet both of these godly men have learned how to be good stewards of their ability. Steve and Mark use their God-giftedness for their Master by periodically traveling to needy areas of the world and using their medical skill in the name of Christ. Steve has visited the Comoros Islands, which is off the coast of Tanzania, and Mark has traveled south to Venezuela.

Carpenters and plumbers are needed to repair homes ravaged by the forces of tornadoes and floods. Counselors are needed when a company lays off its work force. The opportunities to use your ability for Christ are endless. Do not overlook the obvious mission field, the field right in front of you—your workplace. God knew you would be positioned in your current working environment before the world was made. He made you for that position, and He specifically gifted you to represent Him there. Good stewardship requires you to ask the question: How can I use my God-given talents for Him right where I am?

Most of us will never have the opportunity to travel around the world deploying that which God gave us. For the majority of us, the task is to deploy our ability in dedication to God right where we are now. Steve Barrington and Mark Anderson do not wait until their mission trips materialize to use their specialty for Christ. They use their medical practice as a vehicle to share the Lord through their excellent work and the counseling of their patients and employees.

Do you acknowledge the Source of your special talents? Are you developing these gifts? Have you deployed your abilities for the building of the Kingdom? The good steward can answer yes to all of these questions!

Make a list of those activities and abilities that are naturally interesting and compelling to you. Among this list you are likely to find some of your God-given abilities. Reflect on the list and indicate those abilities that you believe are God-given.

Beside those abilities you believe are God-given, list any activity you have undertaken to develop greater skill. Next, list any activity you can think of in which you could engage that would produce greater skill. Prayerfully take action and develop your abilities.

In another column, list how you are using your talent for the building of the Kingdom. Contact your pastor for additional ideas.

In the last column, list how your ability is helping to capture your workplace for Christ.

Stewardship of Resources

Are you a dues-paying member of your church? Many people and even some Christians believe that writing their checks to the church completes their obligation to their faith. Like being a member of the Lions Club or the Rotary Club, some of us think church membership is embodied solely in our financial commitment.

What a tragedy! This worldly view constitutes poor stewardship of our resources, because our resources are much more than our money. Often, writing a check is the easiest course of action, but God looks for good stewards of the resources He places at our disposal. God desires His children to cheerfully and willingly invest His resources in the work of the Kingdom.

Step 1: Acknowledge God as the Owner. "You may say to yourself, 'My power and the strength of my hands have produced this wealth for me.' But remember the LORD your God, for it is he who gives you the ability to produce wealth, and so confirms his covenant, which he swore to your forefathers, as it is today" (Deut. 8:17–18). Moses made this frank declaration in one of his final sermons to the Israelites. Basic human nature would have us take credit for our bank accounts and material possessions, so the advice of Moses is important. It is the Lord that made us and gave us the ability to produce, so the fruit of our production belongs to Him.

Step 2: Invest your resources in godly investments. David Dorsey owns, leases, and sells truck trailers. Most people see truck trailers as a self-helping tool, but David captured a vision of how his work and business product could advance the cause of Christ.

Dorsey invested his God-given resource, a truck trailer, in God's work immediately after the 1993 Midwest flood. Taking the stewardship initiative, David pulled one of his trailers to the parking lot of a shopping center and challenged his community to fill it up with needed supplies. Within a few days the trailer was full of supplies and en route to Saint Louis in the name of the Savior. David acknowledged God's ownership of the trailers by investing them in God's work. Creative investment of our resources in God's work is the goal. Go and give.

Make a list of your assets. Beside each, concisely state how you became its owner. If your analysis does not reveal the presence of God, dig deeper until you find His activity.

Review your checkbook. Is your giving based on faith, or is it based on fear?

List as many possible Kingdom uses you can imagine for each of the resources you listed. Take action to invest, anticipating opportunity.

Pray that the Lord will open a door of opportunity to you.

Stewardship of Relationships

Team building is a fad sweeping the workplace. Today, a company may send employees on dangerous adventures, hoping the experience will bond its people into a cohesive team. Check out some of America's biggest, swiftest corporate "rivers" and you will find rafts full of petrified coworkers clinging to one another. Team building is a concept that recognizes the value and potential of relationships. Team-building exercises attempt to force relationships to develop. The idea is fine, but it falls short when compared to the potential of building relationships in Christ.

What is the mathematical probability of getting to know the specific individuals in your life given the number of people that have lived, the number of people that are living, and the number of people that will live. Billions of people have lived, are living, and will live, yet you are probably surrounded by only several hundred friends and coworkers. My guess is that the probability of interacting with the people you know today cannot be calculated. Do you think your relationships are by chance? No. So why build relationships on negative, river-rapid-induced fear. Why not build your relationships on the positive current of Christ?

Step 1: Look at others through the eyes of Jesus. God created us for eternity. He sewed into each of us special abilities, and He grants to us resources that we are to invest for His benefit. Then God intentionally brings people into our lives to challenge and love us. Our relationships are God-given, and we should place the highest value on them. Jesus told the parable of the lost sheep to illustrate the incalculable value of each of His children. When we are lost, He risks the balance of the herd to find us and bring us back to safety (Matt. 18:10–14). We are challenged to treat others in like manner–and that includes our coworkers. Good stewardship requires that we acknowledge God's role in our relationships and then see others through His eyes.

Step 2: Invest yourself in building relationships. We are required to show the love, encouragement, and forgiveness of Christ. We are to seek and give loving accountability. We should use the time, ability, and resources given to us by our Master in service to those in our path, because ultimately it is the people and our relationships that stand for eternity.

Honey Carter experienced a pain in her back. It was intense and unusual. Her doctor confirmed the worst—cancer. Honey's treatments would be expensive, long, and painful. The pain of her condition and treatments did not concern Honey as much as the expense and time involved.

Honey is a civil servant at Maxwell Air Force Base. She draws a civil servant's pay and is given the standard number of annual sick and vacation days. Since she is not independently wealthy, Honey was concerned about how she would manage.

Treatments began and, as Honey feared, her allotted number of sick and vacation days dwindled. She faced the frightening prospect of taking unpaid leave to complete her treatment. Enter the good stewards. Several of Honey's coworkers realized her need and acted without her knowledge. They rallied the office and donated almost five hundred hours of their vacation time for Honey's use. Her coworkers literally gave up their vacation time at the beach and elsewhere so Honey could complete her treatment without missing a paycheck. They didn't see it as giving up a thing. These workmates considered their vacation time an investment in Honey's life. That is good stewardship of God-given relationships!

❖ Check your appointment book. How much of your time is spent nurturing your relationships?

❖ Make a list of the dominant relationships in your life. Begin praying for each of these people.

❖ Schedule time with these friends over the next two weeks. Tell them you are praying for them.

The Stewardship Stipend

Stewardship has its rewards, but it is not an investment scheme where you give of your resources to God and He gives you an equivalent financial windfall. Someone told me of his stewardship test where he tithed his gross income for a matter of months to see if God would reward him. My friend was very disappointed that an unexpected bonus did not materialize. Unfortunately, too many of us have the mindset that "If I give according to the Old Testament formula, then I will get in return."

Stewardship is a matter of the heart, not the wallet. The Old Testament formula of 10 percent is fine as a guide, but it can mislead. I believe *sacrificial* stewardship of our time, abilities, resources, and relationships is the Christlike model. Time, abilities, resources, and relationships are more than gifts from God. They are God-given tests designed to reveal the condition of our hearts. A heart for God renders sacrificial stewardship.

God honors good stewardship, sacrificial stewardship. Choosing His way does not always lead to financial gain, but His way always leads to eternal spiritual gain. In addition, good stewardship can redeem our prior poor stewardship. Good stewardship leads to the effective use of God's gifts and greater understanding of God's will for our lives.

Redeeming Poor Stewardship

Structures, Inc., failed due to my poor stewardship, but we serve a God that redeems failure. The ministry of Faith at Work, Inc., is benefiting from the lessons I learned through Structures.

God called His people in the Old Testament to be good stewards. They failed. Over and over they failed. How did God respond? He sent Christ to redeem a pattern of poor stewardship.

Maybe you relate to my Structures, Inc., experience. Perhaps you have exercised poor stewardship in the past. Good news! God, through Christ, is ready to redeem.

Using God's Gifts

The builders of the temple, through the development of their skill, knew the people had given enough for the construction. In effect these good stewards of their time, ability, resources, and relationships were telling the people to store up their resources for the next opportunity.

God preprogrammed you with specific abilities, resources, relationships, and time to carry your part of the load in building His earthly civilization and His heavenly kingdom. Good stewardship allows God to work His plan through you.

Understanding God's Will

The Israelites followed God's direction. They constructed the temple just as they had been told. When Moses put the finishing touch on the temple, "Then the cloud covered the Tent of Meeting, and the glory of the Lord filled the tabernacle. Moses could not enter the Tent of Meeting because the cloud had settled upon it, and the glory of the Lord filled the tabernacle. In all the travels of the Israelites, whenever the cloud lifted from above the tabernacle, they would set out; but if the cloud did not lift, they did not set out—until the day it lifted. So the cloud of the Lord was over the tabernacle by day, and fire was in the cloud by night, in the sight of all the house of Israel during all their travels." (Exod. 40:34–38) The cloud was the tangible sign of God's blessing as He used it to show the Israelites the way He wanted them to go.

I have seen that cloud, and I know God's will for me includes reaching out and meshing His message with other lives in the context of the workworld. This clear direction from Him comes as a result of my striving to be a good steward. He has redeemed the Structures debacle and turned that misery into an incredible lesson for many. He has blessed me immeasurably, not with money but with something far more important—a peace that most people do not understand and a glimpse of the eternal difference my life can make following His will.

Do you want to transform your workplace for Christ? Become a student of good stewardship! Dedicate your time, talent, resources, and relationships to the One who owns them, Jesus Christ. Learn to use these God-given assets for His benefit. Then the peace that comes from the redemption of prior poor stewardship will be yours. The contentment and direction of knowing His will for you will become your guide.

10

Integrity
Doing What Is Right Regardless of the Consequences

Warning! The teaching in this chapter is tough. It could lead to radical changes in your life. Self-surgery of your heart can be painful.

Integrity Is from the Heart

Integrity starts in our hearts. Solomon understood the guiding nature and function of our hearts: "Above all else, guard your heart, for it is the wellspring of life" (Prov. 4:23). Solomon also wrote, "As water reflects a face, so a man's heart reflects the man" (Prov. 27:19). Trying to cover the contents of your heart may work for a while, but the words that are truly written on your heart have a way of manifesting themselves in your actions. We can recall the names of people who have fallen because their private lives were inconsistent with their public lives. These people lacked integrity. The heart cries for this virtue, and when it is squashed, the heart eventually overpowers our actions and breaks us.

We could learn from King David's example: "Test me, O LORD, and try me, examine my heart and my mind" (Ps. 26:2). In other words, "Lord, look into my life and convict me of my lack of integrity—now—before the test of adversity overtakes me."

The American Heritage Dictionary of the English Language defines *integrity* as "a steadfast adherence to a moral or ethical code," "the state of being unimpaired," and "the quality or condition of being made whole or undivided." Adhering to God's code and steadfastly standing undivided in the face of adversity is godly integrity. David experienced the test of adversity. He even asked God to test him. David prayed, "I know, my God, that you test the heart and are pleased with integrity" (1 Chron. 29:17).

Are you passing through trials right now? God may be confronting you to find out what is in your heart.

Mike's Test

Mike has always been a hard worker. When he first started working under John, Mike liked his work. After about five months, though, things changed. One day John summoned one of his long-time employees to his office, which was next door to Mike's. In all Mike's days of playing football and basketball and even during his career to that point, Mike had never observed a more demeaning and ugly chewing out than was handed to that unsuspecting employee. The screaming was so bad that an attorney with whom Mike was talking on the phone became speechless until the temper tantrum was over.

Mike was shell-shocked. John's fit of rage violated God's Word. How should Mike respond to the unjustified display of anger? After about two hours, Mike stepped into John's office and told him, "If that is what I have to do to be successful here, then you will have my resignation this afternoon." To Mike's disbelief, John barely remembered the incident; he shrugged it off, telling Mike not to worry about it. Little did Mike know then that the incident and his response to it would serve as a mild test of his integrity for an upcoming spiritual battle.

Over the next few years John and Mike had a number of unpleasant, unnecessary, and ungodly encounters. Not long after the encounter with the longtime employee, John told Mike to change his vacation plans. For a year Mike had been planning to take his family to Disney World, and the trip was just three days away. John did not care, even though he had known of Mike's plans for six months. If Mike wanted to take a vacation, it must come later. Mike and his family adjusted and moved on.

Later, Mike was summoned into John's office and told, "You have been spotted at your daughter's school." True, Mike had eaten lunch with his daughter at school. According to John, eating lunch with your child at school "is not the company way." A light began to flicker in Mike's mind. He knew that his priority and John's priority were not in sync. In response, Mike told John, "My priority in life is God. Family and work flow out of that relationship." Mike went on to explain that his work never suffered due to lack of time invested. That is when John first told Mike that he must segregate his spiritual life from his secular life. Now the battle was clear. Mike was in a war for his very soul.

John's eruptions became so consistent that Mike could practically predict their arrival far in advance. Over the years John's one-sided monologues included some true business issues where the company had stumbled and needed to perform better, but others were business issues where John reacted after receiving about 10 percent of the information necessary to make an informed judgment.

Most of John's intense ramblings were directed at Mike's activities away from the office. Changing vacation dates at the last minute became a ritual. One year Mike's daughter was enrolled in Kamp Kanakuk-Kanakomo in Branson, Missouri.[1] Two days before the family was set to leave for Branson, the vacation dance began. Mike explained the situation to John, who asked, "Can't your daughter go some other time? Your place is here at the office, not on vacation with your family." Once again Mike's battle was defined, and he felt the pressure building up. Mike's wife recruited a friend, and they took off to Branson without him.

Later that year, Mike was summoned into John's office to hear these statements:

- ❖ You have grown so much like Christ that 99 percent of the people here don't understand you. If you intend to lead them, then you must compromise to be more like them.
- ❖ Your friendship with your pastor is a problem for you here because you can't live the way he lives in the real world.
- ❖ What you hear from the pulpit and in Sunday school is not applicable in the real world.

❖ You should not take your children to school in the mornings even if you get to work on time. If you take your children, the people that work here may see you. If they do, then they will know that your wife told you to take the kids. If you do what your wife tells you to do, then you are not in control of your house. If you are not in control of your house, how could you possibly be in control of this company?

❖ Getting angry is a Christlike way to behave. Jesus got angry and threw the people out of the temple. The people got scared of Him, and out of this fear they killed Him.

❖ Satan is making me say these things to you. I have conflict in my soul.

❖ Mike, you have an uncommon peace that I envy because I do not have it.

John professed to be a Christian. Was he really saying these things? Throughout John's speech Mike prayed, "Lord, forgive my insensitivity toward this man. Help me see him as Your creation. Use me to reach him for You. Give me the words I should say." When John finally stopped, Mike asked, "Instead of conforming to the wishes of a band of unbelievers, why don't we show them that my priority of God first, family second, and work third is proper and that not only can we succeed with God in control, we can succeed wildly?" John responded, "Do you really think you can pull all of that off?" Mike, looking John straight in the eye, said, "I cannot do this on my own power but only through the power of Christ." At Mike's response John threw his hands in the air and shook his head. The meeting ended.

Mike stood as a man of integrity, a man whose heart and actions were in sync with God's Word. The easy course of action for Mike would have been to conform to the demands of his employer. Winking at the world, however, would have saddened the Savior, and Mike would have lost his integrity.

Mike's workplace environment is not unique. You, too, may have been oppressed by the tyranny of a worldly boss or coworker, even one who claims to have a relationship with Jesus Christ. The threat of losing your livelihood is among the most difficult life challenges a person can face. When you face such a storm, your integrity is put to the ultimate test.

Organizations and workplaces are not created and endowed with a healthy dose of integrity. This Christlike quality is imported into the workplace by the people who occupy it daily. If you want your workplace to have integrity, integrity must start with you. Mike responded from his heart. He was true to that which he held dear—faith and trust in Jesus Christ. The integrity that described his life had been honed over the years, making Mike ready for the spiritual battle of his life.

Job's Integrity

Mike's story resembles the story of Job; they have a lot in common. Both men experienced tough testing, both were living pictures of integrity. Like Mike, Job remained true to the Word of God, which was written on his heart. Job's test was brutal. He was a wealthy man with a large family consisting of ten children. Job owned seven thousand sheep, three thousand camels, five hundred oxen, and five hundred donkeys. Servants were many and spread over his sprawling estate. "He was the greatest man among all the people of the East" (Job 1:3).

One day, while Job was wisely managing the assets God had given him, Satan made a trip into the presence of God. The Lord asked about Satan's activity and specifically his interest in Job. This piqued Satan's curiosity and he suggested to God, "You have blessed the work of his hands, so that his flocks and herds are spread throughout the land. But stretch out your hand and strike everything he has, and he will surely curse you to your face" (Job 1:10–11). God had enough confidence in Job's integrity to literally hand him over to Satan.

Satan orchestrated the destruction of Job's world. First Job received word that all of his livestock had been killed or stolen. A minute later a messenger reported Job's servants had been killed. Another minute passed and a messenger entered and disclosed Job's children had perished. All ten of his children were gone, and so was his material wealth. Job did not have time to prepare for all of this devastation because all these events occurred within a very short time frame.

Put yourself in Job's shoes for a moment. How would you have responded to this chaos and loss? Imagine yourself in Mike's scenario. How would you have handled his turmoil? Would your friends have said of your response, "I do not blame him for the way he acted. He was dealt a bad hand." Or would those watching you have said, "I am so encouraged by his response. His faith is rock solid!" The difference is integrity, and a model for building integrity into our lives is found in the life of Job.

The story of Job's life begins, "In the land of Uz there lived a man whose name was Job. This man was blameless and upright; he feared God and shunned evil" (Job 1:1). Not only did the writer of this great book attribute those integrity-making qualities to Job, so did God. Speaking to Satan about Job, God said, "There is no one on earth like him; he is blameless and upright, a man who fears God and shuns evil" (Job 1:8). When God describes qualities He likes, we should listen. God attributed these qualities to Job, a man of integrity.

A Person of Integrity Is Blameless

We live in a litigious society. Some people look for any excuse to use the court system as if it were a lottery. The cost to a potential plaintiff is minimal, but the payoff can be substantial, inspiring some people to sue everybody from their own kin to their arch rival. Somewhere in between the two is the employer. In today's society people are suing their employers for a variety of reasons, and this has caused employers to run scared.

Fear of Litigation

Employers have created policies designed to head off potential litigation. Many of these policies are good because they require employees' good behavior. Many of these policies, however, are bad because they limit the building of relationships that can honor God. For example, some companies have stopped the company picnic for fear someone could get hurt and the company would be sued. Further evidence of workplace relationship changes was demonstrated when I spoke with the president of a mid-sized firm. He told me of a pastor who encouraged his employees with a gentle touch on the shoulder. Laughing, this corporate policymaker said, "That pastor does not live in the real world. In the real world you can't touch someone on the shoulder. You will be sued for sexual harassment."

This executive's view is sad but typical among senior management today. In many cases, corporate heads have become obsessed with fear of litigation, causing them to mitigate any circumstance that could appear litigious regardless of the action's potential for good.

Living in fear of being sued is a sad existence. That style of management denies the truth that any of us can be sued for just about anything. The question that needs to be asked in workplaces today is "Are our motivations honorable?" I am not speaking here necessarily of the development and manufacture of a product. Rather, I am probing the question of employee policies and procedures. Could an argument be brought that you or your company are to blame for imposing a policy designed to have a class of employees quit, or would you and your company be found blameless?

Samuel's Example

Blameless living is a matter of the heart. All of us sin, but a God-motivated life behaving in a way that leaves no room for accusation is blameless. When Samuel was about to anoint Saul as king, he asked the people, "Testify against me in the presence of the LORD and his anointed. Whose ox have I taken? Whose donkey have I taken? Whom have I cheated? Whom have I oppressed? From whose hand have I accepted a bribe to make me shut my eyes? If I have done any of these, I will make it right." The people affirmed Samuel's integrity and his blameless life. Then he said, "The LORD is witness against you, and also his anointed is witness this day, that you have not found anything in my hand" (1 Sam. 12:3, 5).

Certainly Samuel sinned during his life, but he lived a blameless life. He left no room for accusation, and the people recognized his life was properly motivated and well lived. I doubt Samuel was too worried that someone would step forward and level a charge. He had the confidence that a blameless life affords. He knew there were no skeletons in his closet. Furthermore, Samuel knew his life would be his best defense if a bogus accusation were made. A false accusation would not stick because Samuel lived a blameless life.

One reason corporate America has become obsessed by the fear of litigation is that much of corporate America is not living a truly blameless life. Too often companies, the men and women who lead them, and their employees are living on the edge, in the gray. Thus the confidence that comes from living blamelessly does not exist. There is concern that past or current actions may create a case where blame could be assessed.

Why can one person offer an encouraging touch on the shoulder and have the recipient appreciate the gesture while another person receiving the same action resents the touch? The answer is found in the life of the encourager up to and including the moment of the encounter. When touched by a life with a reputation for ulterior motives and unspeakable desires, the recipient will rebel. When touched by a life that has lived blamelessly, the receiver's heart leaps with honor and excitement.

Do you have the confidence of Samuel? Are you willing to stand before your coworkers, employees, employers, and customers and ask them to assess your life? As a member of senior management in several companies and having had the opportunity to know and work with senior managers from other companies, I do not believe most people are willing to follow Samuel's lead. If employers and employees alike would become obsessed with living a blameless life, the regressive, paranoid, and defensive mindset of fear of blame would be transformed into a healthy, progressive, and intentional desire to help others grow. A positive outlook comes from living a blameless life, and it is necessary to capture your company for Christ.

❖ No special test is required to determine blameless living. Either you are or you are not, and you know the answer. Have you lived a blameless life? Are there skeletons in your past that cause concern regarding how others may interpret your future actions? Maybe you have had a sordid past but now are seeking to please God with all you have. Are you presently living a blameless life?

❖ God is just to forgive sin, and most people will forgive if you sincerely ask.

❖ As you contemplated the question of blameless living, some areas of question may have come to mind. Make a list of those areas and focus on correcting any questionable behavior.

❖ Ask your accountability partner to work with you on these areas.

A Person of Integrity Is Upright

How did Job respond to the calamity in his life? "At this, Job got up and tore his robe and shaved his head. Then he fell on the ground in worship and said: 'Naked I came from my mother's womb, and naked I will depart. The LORD gave and the LORD has taken away; may the name of the LORD be praised'" (Job 1:20–21). Job worshiped God, demonstrating that he was exactly the man God described as upright. To be upright is to be righteous, to have absolute faith in and commitment to God as you follow Him in obedience. Job could have waved his fist toward heaven and blamed God for his loss. Instead, Job chose to acknowledge and praise God's sovereignty.

Later in the Book of Job we find Satan back in the presence of God. God asked Satan where he had been and, like the earlier exchange, Satan said he had been roaming about. Then God asked about Job. Satan must have been frustrated by Job's godly response to the devastation in his life. This time Satan told God he would torture Job, so Satan afflicted Job with terrible sores from head to toe. Job's wife must have been tired of watching Job praise God in the midst of their horrific circumstances. She replied to the sores saying, "Are you still holding on to your integrity? Curse God and die!" (Job 2:9).

Imagine you are in the midst of a job-related crisis. You muster all the energy you can find to hold on to your integrity. You come home, expecting your spouse to affirm your faithfulness and encourage you to press on. Instead, you are told to curse God. The one person in the world who should stand by you and undergird you with confidence pulls the rug out. Your spouse withdraws her support from you. How would you handle that situation? You could take the easy road and give in to your spouse's wish. Better yet, you could follow Job's example saying, "You are talking like a foolish woman. Shall we accept good from God, and not trouble?" (Job 2:10). Job's faith, commitment, and obedience won. Job remained righteous and upright.

Job had friends, well-meaning but sadly mistaken friends. Satan had used Job's wife to tempt him to blame God. Now he used several of Job's friends to counsel Job and turn him against God. Once again imagine you are in the midst of a crisis. You probably are not thinking clearly. It is natural to rely on friends for advice. However, while the advice your friends dispense is well intended, it is off base. Following their guidance would lead to a breach of your integrity. Perhaps you should follow Job's lead. "I will never admit you are in the right; till I die, I will not deny my integrity. I will maintain my righteousness and never let go of it; my conscience will not reproach me as long as I live" (Job 27:5–6). These were Job's good words for his unwise counselors. Are you willing to look silly in the eyes of your friends? Job's friends must have thought he was crazy, but sometimes appearing silly and crazy in the world's eyes is necessary to remain righteous and upright in the eyes of God.

How do you respond to the calamities of life, particularly at work? The world needs Christians to stand upright. Your workplace needs Christians to stand upright. Your workplace needs *you* to stand upright.

❖ Write down the details of a crisis in your life and how you responded. Did your actions acknowledge your commitment to Christ? How would you rate your integrity in that circumstance?

❖ Make a list of the most difficult recurring problems in your work. Beside each entry, note what actions you can take that will develop your commitment to God and reveal your faith in Him.

A Person of Integrity Fears God

When a person encounters the living God, fear overtakes him. This fear is not the kind you feel when you see a horror movie or the evening news. This fear is a special awe and respect for God. Unlike the fear induced by terror that causes you to run, this fear drives you to your knees. It compels you to hide your face, because the face of God is holy. It induces you to praise Him. Job immediately fell to the ground and praised God.

When your integrity is challenged, what is your perspective? Do you hunker down and arm yourself with the verbal equivalent of a hand grenade? Do you plot out exactly how you will snare the one with whom you are having the conflict? If you want to honor God and capture your workplace for Christ, you must fix your perspective. The proper perspective flows from your fear of God, and it acknowledges that the battle belongs to the Lord.

Job did not lash out at anyone during his trouble. He did not point the finger at God or his friends because, I believe, Job had the proper perspective–the "God-owns-it-all-and-this-is-His-battle" perspective. Job's respect for God translated into his acknowledging God's ownership of everything, including the tough times. David shared that perspective. He also respected God so much that he left the ownership of his battles to Him.

Even as a child, David feared God. The Philistines had challenged the Israelites to battle. The lines were drawn. The armies were positioned and out stepped a Philistine named Goliath. Goliath stood nine feet tall and was armed from head to toe. The Israelites trembled in fear as Goliath cursed them. Day after day Goliath came out and challenged the Israelites, but no one from the opposing army stepped forward to fight.

David's older brothers were among the Israelites. One day their father, Jesse, sent David to deliver food to his sons. David saw Goliath but was not afraid. He gathered up a few stones, took his slingshot, and marched out to the battle line. Goliath laughed him off. David had the next laugh as he took a stone and, with the aid of his sling, buried the stone in the forehead of Goliath.

God truly had the last laugh, because David acted out of his fear of God, acknowledging God's ownership of the fight. "David said to the Philistine, 'You come against me with sword and spear and javelin, but I come against you in the name of the LORD Almighty, the God of the armies of Israel, whom you have defied. . . . All those gathered here will know that it is not by the sword or spear that the LORD saves; for the battle is the LORD's, and he will give all of you into our hands" (1 Sam. 17:45, 47).

It took a child to teach the adults an important truth. It took the small in stature to teach the giant fear of God. It took the weak to teach the strong the proper perspective. What will it take for you? Do you truly have a healthy fear of God, a respect that allows Him to own it all, including your adversity? The time to develop such respect for God is before a crisis sweeps you off your feet.

❖ Reread the testimony you wrote earlier as you studied chapter 8. Since the time you accepted Christ as your Savior, has your respect for Him grown?

❖ Look again at the writing you completed about a crisis in your life. What did your actions reveal about your respect for God and your acknowledging His ownership of everything, including adversity?

❖ Pray that God will help you give your adversity to Him.

A Person of Integrity Shuns Evil

I heard Chuck Swindoll say once, "If you have to do the wrong thing to stay on the team, then you are on the wrong team. Either change the team or get off of it!" Investment banking is a business built around a transaction or a deal. It may be the merger of two companies or the issuance of stock for a single company. When a transaction like this occurs, the investment banker brings together a group of professionals that includes bankers, attorneys, and financial analysts. The group then functions as a team to conclude the transaction.

During my investment banking career I had the opportunity to be a part of a number of unique and exciting projects. Among them was a project involving the National Aeronautics and Space Administration, better known as NASA. A plant owned by the manufacturer of a space shuttle component literally blew up soon after the shuttle program began to accelerate. I was contacted and asked to put together a team to meet with company and NASA officials to discuss financing the rebuilding of the manufacturing plant.

Among the team I had assembled was a representative of a foreign bank who I did not know until this project gave us the occasion to meet. The project was time-consuming, requiring travel to NASA headquarters and the site of the proposed construction. Day and night we worked to structure our proposal. This project required approximately five hundred million dollars to complete. If completed, my firm would be paid a fee of approximately five million dollars, and my share would be approximately two million dollars.

One day I received a call from the representative of the foreign bank. He informed me that his bank was close to approving their participation in the project, but there was one small snag. It seemed he needed ten thousand dollars in cash to complete the approval process and needed me to bring it to him personally. "Oh," I responded, "if you guys have incurred legal fees and want us to pay them in advance of the closing of the deal, we can do that. Our firm will send a check to your bank." But that did not seem to be the problem. The more we discussed the subject, the more I realized this man and some of his fellow bankers wanted a little payola for their participation. "No way" were the only words that formed in my mouth. Never before had I been confronted with a bribe. Not only was this astonishing, it was devastating. My refusal was followed by the slamming of the phone. I never called the bank official back. The deal died, and so did my dream of two million dollars. It may have been easy to justify a ten-thousand-dollar "investment" for a return of two million dollars, but I knew this was wrong and dishonoring to God.

I was on the wrong team, and in that instance change was not an option; I had to get off the team. Shun evil. Run. Paul admonished Timothy to flee the trap of pursuing wealth (1 Tim. 6:11). That is exactly what I did. Now, looking back with a level head, I praise God. I felt cleansed and gained spiritual energy as a result of that exercise of shunning evil.

Job shunned evil. When Satan afflicted Job with those unsightly sores, Job took action to get rid of them. "Job took a piece of broken pottery and scraped himself with it as he sat among the ashes" (Job 2:8). Running from evil is often an unpleasant and painful process. To truly distance ourselves from sin, we may have to walk away from great material gain, get a new set of friends, or even find a new job. But the result is an energetic cleansing.

❖ Are you facing an ethical dilemma at work? Are you torn because the potential payoff is so great and the necessary compromise seems so insignificant? Welcome to the world of integrity. Prayerfully study the Book of Job.

❖ Next, write the details of the dilemma, the people involved and the circumstances. Craft a God-honoring response on paper before you enter the situation again. This will make your communication effective and compelling.

❖ Maybe you are not facing an overt crisis at work now. You will. Prepare for the crisis in advance by studying the Book of Job, the account of the temptation of Christ (Matt. 4:1–11), and the last week of the life of Christ (Matt. 21-27; Mark 11-15; Luke 19:28–23:56; and John 12–19). Note your impressions of how Job and Christ shunned evil.

God's Promise for Men and Women of Integrity

And now the rest of the story about Mike. He was in a crisis. His job, his livelihood, was on the line. One of Mike's great difficulties with the situation was that John rarely exploded over issues related to the business. Furthermore, John was not correcting Mike because of unbecoming or objectionable conduct. Mike was in conflict with his boss because Mike was an intentional Christian. John did not like Mike anymore than Goliath liked David. Since Mike was blameless, the only strategy John could develop was to attack the very core of Mike's heart, his faith.

After several years of working with John, praying for him, suggesting they study the Bible together, and striving to help John see the light, Mike knew he had come to a fork in the road. Mike told John one last time that his priorities in life would not change and that God would stay at the top. The situation remained the same: to stay on the team Mike would have to conform to the worldly wishes of John. The decision was clear; though he had worked for change, the time had come for Mike to get off the team.

Walking away from a big salary and the prestige of a senior position in a large company is tough, but sometimes it is necessary if we are to maintain our integrity and do what is right, regardless of the consequences. Each day presents a new challenge as Mike and his family look to the future. Nevertheless, Mike has found God to be faithful as he and his family stand on God's promises to people of godly integrity, which include being guarded, guided, and undergirded.

We Are Guarded

Solomon said, "Righteousness guards the man of integrity, but wickedness overthrows the sinner" (Prov. 13:6). "He whose walk is blameless is kept safe, but he whose ways are perverse will suddenly fall" (Prov. 28:18). Christians enjoy eternal life the minute they accept the Savior. When we are in Christ, our earthly perspective is transformed by a heavenly directive. During a crisis, when our integrity is challenged, nonbelievers cannot understand how we can go forward. As Solomon said, we are protected. Satan can throw everything he has at us, and those barbs might sting. But the pain is temporary, because through Christ we have overcome the world.

How has Mike coped with being out of work? God rallied His people around Mike. Through the love and care of fellow Christians, God has insulated and guarded him and his family.

We Are Guided

"The integrity of the upright guides them, but the unfaithful are destroyed by their duplicity" (Prov. 11:3). To the Christian, I believe this means to follow your heart. Let your heart be your guide; then your actions will reflect what is written there.

Mike was guided by his integrity. The easy route for him would have been to compromise and follow his boss. Instead, he let his heart lead him. He responded in a Christlike way, which resulted in a major career change. Nonetheless, Mike knew he was guarded by God. As he drove home after his resignation and pondered how to tell his family of the enormous change in their lives, Mike felt the guidance of God. God would not lead him to waste this experience. But how could Mike use this circumstance for Christ? After he and his wife discussed the happenings, they gathered their children together and gently disclosed the news. The children wanted to know how it would affect their world. Then, as a family, they read the Bible and prayed together. Mike lived out the point that in adversity we go to God. God guided Mike to use his circumstance as an eternal teaching tool with his family. We, too, can be confident that when we follow Christ, He will lead us.

We Are Undergirded

"The man of integrity walks securely, but he who takes crooked paths will be found out" (Prov. 10:9). Have you ever walked along a beach and felt the sand slip under your feet? Maybe you have walked through a marsh. While fishing in Alaska, I traveled by foot over a marsh. Each step sank about four inches. The ground under me was not firm; it was not secure. As a result I walked attentively.

Walking in integrity with Christ is a rock solid jaunt. The ground does not slip under your feet. You can walk briskly, knowing the foundation on which you tread is secure. Our foundation for life is found in Christ. We can live securely, knowing the Word He has given us is true. We can face adversity with the assurance that the Counselor is with us.

If you have maintained your integrity in the face of adversity, you know the truth of this proverb. Maybe you faced adversity but left your integrity behind. Unfortunately, you, too, may know the truth of the proverb because you have been "found out." There is hope in Christ. He does forgive. Take His free offer of grace. Walk securely.

What will be the legacy of your life? Will you spend your days working for some temporal treasure with one foot in the world and the other in your faith? Will you live with a divided heart? Christ said that is impossible. "No one can serve two masters. Either he will hate the one and love the other, or he will be devoted to the one and despise the other. You cannot serve both God and Money" (Matt. 6:24). Integrity demands that we stay true to our hearts. We are to live a blameless life, upright before God. We must show God our most reverent respect. When Satan comes, run! God has much to give His faithful servant who does what is right regardless of the circumstances.

PART

2

Five Steps to Implanting Christ in Your Workplace

11

Get on Your Knees
Step 1

Your workplace cannot be transformed for Christ unless and until you fall to your knees in prayer. The battle for the hearts and minds of your coworkers belongs to God. The power to represent Him comes as you know His will and as you allow Him to change you. Knowledge of His will and experiencing Christlike change come through the work of prayer. "Call to me and I will answer you and tell you great and unsearchable things you do not know" (Jer. 33:3).

Guy Doud's Day

Guy Doud sought to transform his workplace for Christ. Doud was a schoolteacher from Minnesota who started his day of work by calling on the Creator. I heard Mr. Doud say, during the course of a speech, that he so wanted to impact his kids for Christ that he would sit in their desks before school and intercede on their behalf.

Doud started with step 1, prayer. There in the presence of God, Guy Doud performed his toughest and most important work. It was in that prayerful mode that he won his workplace, his classroom, for Christ. Through his communication with God, He continuously understood his role in the will of the Father. Also through his communication with God, Guy Doud was continuously changed to meet the challenge of those God directed to him.

Guy Doud found that God changes us through our prayer. High-school teachers encounter some tough, unlovable kids. Day after day

Doud met these unmotivated teenagers and attempted to change their lives. The rigors of such continual daily contact could easily harden a person's perspective. How did Doud respond? He picked a place of prayer, the kid's desks, and regularly and repetitively prayed for them. How did Doud's prayer partner, the almighty God, respond? God changed this teacher's perspective about the kids and kept him in the Christ-honoring mode of loving his students. Maybe that is why Guy Doud was selected National Teacher of the Year in 1986.

Prayer is the first step toward capturing our workplaces for Christ because we are on God's turf, working His plan, and He must direct our efforts. We must communicate with our Commander and grow in the knowledge of Christ. This is a dynamic process that requires us to change.

It happened with Jesus' disciples. In all the time Christ spent with them, the Twelve specifically asked Him to teach them only one thing—how to pray. "One day Jesus was praying in a certain place. When he finished, one of his disciples said to him, 'Lord, teach us to pray, just as John taught his disciples'" (Luke 11:1). This example of the disciples and our Lord teaches that prayer is vital to the Christian life.

What about your prayer life? How did you first communicate with God? It wasn't through a memo or an E-mail message. It was through prayer that you first began your walk with God. Prayer was the commencement exercise of your faith. Prayer was the commencement exercise of my faith and the faith of all believers. Prayer should be the commencement exercise of all of our endeavors.

The Prayer Life of Jesus

If you wrote down what you did yesterday, would you include your morning shower or how you started your car? Probably not. Those actions come so naturally that they are usually viewed as insignificant. For Christ, prayer was so natural and common to His daily activities that the Gospel writers could have overlooked this very important area of His life. Christ lived a pattern of prayer. He established a routine of regular communication, but His prayer life was so significant that excluding His many communications with the Father would have materially misrepresented the events of His day.

Matthew records that Jesus "went up into the hills by himself to pray" just before He called Peter out of the boat and onto the water (Matt. 14:23). When the children were brought to Him, Jesus placed His hands on them and prayed (Matt. 19:13–15). In crisis our Lord prayed. Speaking to His disciples in the Garden of Gethsemane, Jesus said, "Sit here while I go over there and pray" (Matt. 26:36). After healing many, He rested; then "very early in the morning, while it was still dark, Jesus got up, left the house and went off to a solitary place, where he prayed" (Mark 1:35).

In crisis and in good times Jesus prayed. For the physically sick and for the spiritually sick, Jesus prayed. For the disciples and for each one of us, Jesus prayed. "He looked toward heaven and prayed: . . . 'My prayer is not only for them alone. I pray also for those who will believe in me through their message'" (John 17:1, 20). On that day so many years ago, Jesus actually prayed for you and me.

The prayers of Christ reveal several patterns we can acknowledge and follow. Jesus established a place of prayer, a frequency of prayer, and a form of prayer.

The Place of Jesus' Prayer

Mark spoke of a solitary place where Jesus prayed. Matthew cited the mountainside as His venue. Luke records, "Jesus went out as usual to the Mount of Olives, and his disciples followed Him. On reaching the place, he said to them, 'Pray that you will not fall into temptation'" (Luke 22:39–40). Notice the wording in Luke's account, "Jesus went out *as usual* to the Mount of Olives." This place was not foreign to Jesus or His disciples. The Mount of Olives was one place, I believe, among several where Jesus prayed regularly. Luke states even more emphatically, "But Jesus often withdrew to lonely places and prayed" (Luke 5:16).

❖ Jesus established specific places for prayer, solitary and lonely places. Guy Doud established a special place of prayer, the desks of his students. Where do you pray? Do you have a special place where you meet God? Perhaps a room in your house is your solitary place for communion with God. The room needs to be out of the flow of family traffic. You should locate a spot that can be visited almost any time of the day or night. Maybe you prefer to be outside where you can experience God's gentle breeze or rising sun. Pick a place that can become your personal place with God. A solitary place. A place of comfortable communion with God. A place where distractions do not compete for your attention. A place to focus on God. Guy Doud found that unique setting at his pupils' desks during the quiet morning hours. Where is your solitary place?

❖ Find a solitary place where you can pray without distractions.

❖ Obtain a Rolodex card holder and an individual Rolodex card for each of your coworkers. On each card place the name of one coworker.

The Frequency of Jesus' Prayer

Maintaining a consistent and continuous prayer life is difficult. Today our schedules are jam-packed with activities, and most of us have difficulty staying with the routine of prayer.

I wonder if Jesus felt a time crunch? Imagine a day in the life of the Lord. He has just healed someone, and the person hurries to proclaim the good news. Do you think the masses of humanity hearing this revelation would not run after Him? Do you think He was not in great demand? I believe Christ felt the crunch of time running out each day. Still, He always made time for prayer.

There are a number of references to the prayers of Christ in the Gospels, and no doubt Christ prayed more often than was recorded. In addition to modeling frequent prayer, Jesus taught the disciples directly. "Then Jesus told his disciples a parable to show them that they should *always* pray and not give up" (Luke 18:1, emphasis added). Notice that Jesus told the disciples to pray always, continually and continuously. Paul encouraged the Thessalonians saying, "We *constantly* pray for you" (2 Thess. 1:11, emphasis added). He also admonished them to "pray continually" (1 Thess. 5:17).

The teaching of our Savior is clear. Paul learned the discipline of frequent prayer, employed it in his own life, and taught it to those under his leadership. Now the task is ours to assess our prayer periods. "But," you say, "we just established the need for a special, solitary, lonely place for prayer. There is no way I can pray continually in that place, because I have to go to work and be at home and other places."

True, it would be impossible to remain in one place continually for prayer unless we lived in a convent or monastery. Even in those places there is work to be done. So how do we pray continually? Christ modeled a pattern of frequent prayer both in a special place and in other places as well.

I have a friend who prays very early every morning in his living room. That is his special, solitary place. Then during the day he offers short, silent prayers in his car, his office, the elevator, the hallway, and anywhere he feels prompted to hurl his concerns heavenward. That is continual, constant prayer. Intense praise, intercession, and petition at a designated time in a special place, punctuated with frequent prayers at other times.

Christ teaches us to continuously communicate with God. Christ also teaches that repeated prayer is a discipline God appreciates.

Jesus told a parable of a widow and a ruthless judge. The judge did not fear God or care about other people. A widow came to the judge asking him to grant her justice against her adversary. The judge refused again and again, but the widow persisted. Eventually the judge said to himself, "'Even though I don't fear God or care about men, yet because this widow keeps bothering me, I will see that she gets justice, so that she won't eventually wear me out with her coming!' And the Lord said, 'Listen to what the unjust judge says. And will not God bring about justice for his chosen ones, who cry out to him day and night? Will he keep putting them off? I tell you, he will see that they get justice, and quickly'" (Luke 18:4–8). God responds to repeated prayer; that is why Luke said, "They should always pray and not give up" (Luke 18:1).

Repeated prayer is a challenge. My tendency is to voice my prayer and wait. During one trying season of my life I allowed anger to build in me. Frustrated and mad, I asked God to forgive me for harboring the anger and to deliver me from it. Then I waited, and I waited. But the anger did not go away. In fact, I felt even more angry about my circumstance than when I had prayed about it weeks before. *Where is God?* I thought.

In that valley, God taught me to leave my burden at the Cross. God could have granted my request for deliverance after that first prayer, but He didn't. Instead, God used that trial to teach me the discipline of repeated prayer. I found freedom from the anger that had engulfed me as I met with God daily and discussed my problem. Over and over, I deposited my burden at the Cross, and God changed me.

How frequently do you pray? We need a special place to pray, and we need to develop the discipline to pray there regularly and repeatedly.

❖ Determine a time in your schedule when you can shut out the noise of the world and focus on communication with God. Build your calendar around your time with God.

❖ Using the Rolodex cards bearing the name of each coworker, make notes about needs in their lives. Pray regularly and repeatedly for those needs. Write on the card when God answers your prayer.

❖ Add a Rolodex card for any workplace concerns. For example, make a card to remind you to pray for your effort to capture your workplace for Christ. Make another card to prompt you to pray that the other believers in your work-world will be challenged by your witness and compelled to partner with you as you capture your workplace for Christ.

The Form of Jesus' Prayer

When the disciples asked Jesus to teach them to pray He responded saying, "Father, hallowed be your name, your kingdom come. Give us each day our daily bread. Forgive us our sins, for we also forgive everyone who sins against us. And lead us not into temptation" (Luke 11:2–4).

This prayer is commonly called the model prayer. Bible scholars have divided this prayer into five classic sections: praise, surrender, dependence, forgiveness, and protection.

I like the Lord's form of His model prayer. It gives us structure and cohesion without limiting spontaneity when we pray. This form helps us communicate with God, and it helps God communicate with us.

Praise

Christ's model for prayer begins with praise: "Father, hallowed be your name" (Luke 11:2). In essence, Christ was acknowledging the holiness of God. If we are sensitive to God, acknowledging His holiness, purity, goodness, and creativity is the only way to initiate

An Example of a Workplace Prayer

Lord, You are an awesome and creative God. Each day brings a new, changed world for us to explore. I am overwhelmed by Your creativity as I look around my office and see the people You have made for me to know through my work. All of us blend together to use the unique talents You have given us to produce something excellent.

Oh God, may we work in Your name. May our work, my work, be used for Your good purpose. Lord, You said through Your prophet Jeremiah, "For I know the plans I have for you, . . . plans to prosper you and not to harm you, plans to give you hope and a future" (Jer. 29:11). Lord, I know You have a great plan for me, and I have no need to fully know it now. All I want to do is give this work over to You. Lord, You are the Creator of my work, and I thank You for it.

Lord, as I give You my work today, it scares me. I know I must depend on You, and I know You will meet all of my needs. So change any attitude in me that gets in the way of my dependence on You. Lord, thank You that You are sufficient to meet my needs.

Forgive me, Lord, when my attitude does not honor You. Forgive me when my attitude and actions suggest I am in control. Lord, You are in control. Lord, forgive me for my insensitivity to Bob's problem yesterday. That was an opportunity to express Your love to him, and I failed. Lord, make my heart sensitive so I can always portray Your love and encouragement and forgiveness to my coworkers.

And now, Lord, as I attempt to capture my workplace for You, please protect me from Satan's attack. Lord, teach me through Your Word how I should do my job and work with those in my path. Protect me, too, Lord, by softening the hearts of those You would have me meet in Your name. Lord, You are my protector; You are my everything. In the name of Jesus, Amen.

communication with Him. Praising God is the appropriate way to address Him when we pray, especially about our workworld.

In your current circumstance you may wonder where God is active in your workplace. You may work for a tyrant or with nonbelievers whose only ambition is to make it to payday so they can party the weekend away. You wonder where the God of all creation is in the midst of this chaos.

You may be asking yourself, "Why should I thank God for being able to work around here?" Here's a list:

- ❖ Thank God for work itself. No matter how difficult or mundane, work is a gift from God. See Ecclesiastes 2:24 and Genesis 2:15.
- ❖ Thank God for your coworkers. Like you, they are created in the image of God.
- ❖ Thank God for giving you a sensitive and caring heart that compels you to capture your workplace and your coworkers for Christ.
- ❖ Thank God for providing for your needs through your work.
- ❖ Thank God for using your work to give you knowledge that is helpful to build His kingdom.

Perhaps you can think of more reasons to praise God for your work.
Surrender

Through our praise we acknowledge God as the Creator and Owner of everything. Naturally, then, we surrender everything to its rightful owner. "Your kingdom come" were the words Christ used to describe our surrender to God (Luke 11:2). Our entire life is about pursuing God and allowing Him to bring about a radical Christlikeness in us. God can accomplish His purpose in us when we surrender our will to His will. That transformation should be evident in all areas of our lives, including work.

So when you pray, surrender your work to Him. He created your work to bring about good in your life. Allow God to use it for His purpose. As you raise the white flag of surrender, add those attitudes and self-directed purposes of your work such as a desire for wealth, prestige, status, and position. Surrender your desires, hopes, and dreams to those of the Father.

Dependence

Now, having surrendered everything in your workworld to the Creator, you must acknowledge your dependence on Him. "Give us each day our daily bread" (Luke 11:3). True surrender is necessary for you to truly acknowledge and act on your dependence on Him. So, if you find you are continuing to focus on the abundance in life rather than the necessary, go back to surrender and pray frequently and repeatedly that God will change your attitude so you can surrender all of your work to Him.

Living a fully surrendered life means you no longer depend on your job to supply your needs; you now depend on God for everything. Your perspective must shift from your company to God. He uses your work to provide the necessities of life. He may even choose to change your work venue. If you depend on your work and your employer to provide the necessities, then your perspective may cause you to miss God's leading.

For almost sixteen years I worked in the banking industry. After years of hard work, I landed in the number two job of a large financial institution. Life was good. Then one day God spoke and told me to leave the banking world and finish this book. If my perspective had been fixed on the company, if I had surrendered all to the board of directors, then my response to God's prompting may have been, "Well, Lord, after I finish this book, what will I do for a living? You do know I depend on this job to meet my needs and wants?" But confronted with God's activity in my life, I asked myself, "What am I really living for? On whom do I really depend?" I have always testified that I live for God and depend on Him. God confronted me and challenged me to surrender everything to Him, including my work, and live in dependence on Him.

When I took this step of surrendering everything to Christ, I had to get rid of two of my favorite slogans:

> If it is to be, it is up to me.
> Look out for number one.

Our culture rewards those who buy into the worldly perspective and depend on it. While my family's new life of greater dependence on God has its ups and downs, I tell you that God does provide at just the right time. The trek of following Him is more joyous than any we have traveled.

Forgiveness

We have praised God for creating everything, especially our work. We have surrendered it all to Him, including our work, and we have acknowledged our dependence on Him to meet our needs. Out of our dependence we acknowledge our need for forgiveness. Since God created and owns everything, He alone can forgive. "Forgive us our sins, for we also forgive everyone who sins against us" (Luke 11:4). We must petition God for forgiveness, and we must forgive.

Have you checked your attitude around the office lately? Do you personify the Christlike characteristics of love, encouragement, forgiveness, balanced living, accountability, excellence, communication, keeping your promises, stewardship, and integrity? Our goal is to grow in our likeness of Christ, and when we fall short we need forgiveness. Maybe you have been slacking off and not giving a Christlike effort. Perhaps you have undercut a coworker in an attempt to get ahead. Maybe you are like many of us who have shut God out of the work He created for us. If so, ask God to forgive you and give you the courage to grow beyond your sin.

Rob owns a small business. One of his employees stole over four thousand dollars from him. How did Rob respond? He went to God for direction and asked for the grace to forgive his fallen employee. Then Rob confronted the employee saying, "I forgive you because I have been forgiven." Only God could have given Rob such a Christlike attitude. Perhaps someone has wronged you. Ask God to forgive you for sin, and ask God to help you forgive others who wrong you.

Protection

"And lead us not into temptation" (Luke 11:4). Christ ends His model prayer by acknowledging God as our Protector and asking for a shield from the enemy. You may wonder why you need protection. Satan will not sit by and allow you to capture your workplace for Christ unhindered. You *will* meet Satan as you move ahead on behalf of God. You need God to protect you from Satan's obstacles. Maybe Satan will attack your mind and fill it with doubt about God's promise of provision. Maybe Satan will attempt to disrupt your relationships. Perhaps His attack will come as you attempt to grow more in likeness to Christ by living out the ten Christlike principles. Whatever Satan's method, you need God's protection.

❖ Right now, pause and pray for your coworkers and your effort to capture your workplace for Christ following the model given to us by Christ.

❖ After you have prayed, write your prayer so you do not forget the needs that surfaced. Let this prayer be the beginning of your prayer journal.

Praying as Partners with God

Prayer is two-way communication. It is a partnership. We voice our praise, surrender, dependence, petition for pardon, and plea for protection to God, and He answers. God hears our prayers, and God answers us. Through prayer God changes us and equips us for His tasks.

God Hears our Prayers

I know God hears our prayers because He said He does. He also gives us real, tangible answers at just the right time—His time. "If my people, who are called by my name, will humble themselves and pray and seek my face and turn from their wicked ways, then I will hear from heaven and will forgive their sin and will heal their land" (2 Chron. 7:14). The Lord made that statement to Solomon, and God continues to honor His promise today.

In your special place of regular and repeated prayer, remember the condition God attached to His promise. We must approach God sincerely, humbly, with a deep desire to know God, and we must turn from the sin that blocks our communion with God. When we pray with this attitude and resolve, God promises to hear us. We can rest easy and walk confidently that our prayers are heard.

God Answers Our Prayers

"Confess your sins to each other and pray for each other so that you may be healed. The prayer of a righteous man is powerful and effective. Elijah was a man just like us. He prayed earnestly that it would not rain, and it did not rain on the land for three and a half years. Again he prayed, and the heavens gave rain, and the earth produced its crops" (James 5:16–18). James proclaims that prayer is powerful and effective. He then follows his claim with the evidence found in the life of Elijah.

Think about how God has answered your prayers. Maybe God told you *no* because He knew receiving your request would be harmful to you. Maybe God said *go* because your request was timed to coincide with His will for you. Perhaps, however, God said nothing at all. If that is your frustration, understand God is telling you to wait. Take it slowly. He will give you the definitive answer in His perfect time. God will not answer your prayer until He changes you.

God Changes Us through Prayer

Elijah was an ordinary person, like you and me. But he was a man totally surrendered to God, and God answered His prayers. Total surrender, the kind of surrender Elijah demonstrated by following God's directive to an isolated place where the flesh-eating ravens supplied his need for food, is unnatural for us. It is unnatural for me.

I am an average person who is seeking to know God. I have prayed for almost twenty years that the Lord would allow me to use the talents He has given me to creatively follow Him in vocational ministry. On many occasions I felt close to the "answer." Then life moved on and my future appeared to be in banking. I really did not understand why I felt such a desire for vocational ministry while I held such a good job in the world of banking.

One day while fishing the Carluk River in Alaska, God spoke to me in an unmistakable way. He told me, "You have been casting your lure for a ministry in places that were your idea of ministry. Go home and drop your net right where you are!" My ministry was right under my nose, among my coworkers. When God changed my perspective about ministry, He changed me.

I went back home determined to capture my workplace for Christ. I developed a ministry among my coworkers. Out of that ministry the Lord answered my regular and repeated prayer for an opportunity to follow Him creatively by commissioning this book. God does answer our prayers, but He must change us first so we will be equipped for the answer.

You need to pray before you can transform your workplace for Christ. You need to allow God to change you so He can answer your prayer to be used in your place of employment. If you follow the model prayer offered by Christ, God will change you, and He will give you a ministry, a ministry to capture your workplace for Christ.

12

Evaluate the Needs
Step 2

Walter was a clerk in the servicing department of the mortgage company. The servicing department is the area that accepts your mortgage payment, processes the payment, attempts to collect late payments, handles escrow accounts, and performs many other functions. This is a paper-intensive area, where the workers sit and process their work all day.

Walter developed a back problem and asked if the company could provide a different chair for him. The chair he needed provided better support for his back because the back extended slightly higher than the chair he was using at that time. The new chair was approved and delivered several days later. Walter felt a difference almost immediately. Unfortunately, the different feeling was not limited to the comfort of the new chair. Walter's coworkers began to express different feelings–bad feelings.

As amazing as it may seem, insignificant things such as the height of a desk chair or the height of an overhead bookshelf for a desk or even the number of drawers or doors of that overhead bookshelf become the status symbols of the workplace. Walter was provided a desk chair slightly higher than his coworkers' desk chairs, so his once-friendly colleagues turned on him. Walter's associates excluded him from conversation and break time. They even complained that Walter was getting preferential treatment.

I have seen hundreds of Walters. One employee complains that another has "unfairly" received something of value, something like a slightly taller chair.

Pettiness, jealousy, and self-centeredness hamper today's workplace. Day after day I am confronted by the character void that exists in many people. The real need is not the size of the chair. The real need is the empty space where character resides. People do not need tall chairs, they need character. They need Christlike character.

Instead of becoming frustrated by the pettiness and lack of concern expressed by your coworkers, see their need. Instead of retaliating when someone attempts to step on you, see his need. Instead of booting someone out because you are tired of dealing with her continual efforts to get her way, see her need. See the need for Christ and His character.

Developing an attitude that looks beyond a person's fault to see their true need is hard. This attitude comes through the hard work of step 1, prayer. God alone can change you to see the needs of your workplace through His eyes. The needs of your coworkers abound. All around you are lives cracked and broken from the difficulties of life. In your midst walk people who behave strangely, who are rude and ungodly because of their deep need for love, encouragement, and forgiveness. Do not be content to accept a person's poor performance or behavior. Look deeper. Separate the perceived need from the true need. Be a rebuilder of the cracked walls around you.

Stop, Look, and Listen!

A builder's work begins with an inspection of the construction site. Nehemiah was a builder for all time. The account of the rebuilding of the wall around Jerusalem provides instruction for us as we seek to rebuild the cracked lives of our coworkers.

Nehemiah traveled to Jerusalem from Susa. "I went to Jerusalem, and after staying there three days I set out during the night with a few men" (Neh. 2:11–12). What was Nehemiah's first action? He rested and prayed. Nehemiah had been in Jerusalem three days before he set out to inspect the walls. He modeled step 1; he prayed. As you rest and pray, ask God to reveal the true needs of your workplace. Ask God to give you a passion to help those in your workplace find the true answer to their needs.

After Nehemiah had participated with God in prayer, he set out to inspect the cracked walls of Jerusalem. "I had not told anyone what my God had put in my heart to do for Jerusalem. There were no mounts with me except the one I was riding on. By night I went out through the Valley Gate toward the Jackal Well and the Dung Gate, examining the walls of Jerusalem, which had been broken down, and its gates, which had been destroyed by fire. Then I moved on toward the Fountain Gate and the King's Pool, but there was not enough room for my mount to get through; so I went up the valley by night, examining the wall. Finally, I turned back and reentered through the Valley Gate. The officials did not know where I had gone or what I was doing, because as yet I had said nothing to the Jews or the priests or nobles or officials or any others who would be doing the work" (Neh. 2:12–16).

The Stealth Inspection

During the inspection phase of this rebuilding project Nehemiah kept his plans quiet. As you begin inspecting your work-place through the eyes of Jesus, you should keep quiet about what you are doing. I say this for three reasons:

1. This is a time to "be still." Let God reveal the needs around you.
2. Others will mask their behavior if they know you are watching. You must discover their true need.
3. Your intentions may cause misunderstanding among your peers. Some people will incorrectly see your effort as an attempt to browbeat your colleagues.

Capturing your workplace for Christ is about serving those in your workworld, not beating them up for Christ. Understanding the needs of your coworkers and your workplace will enable you to artic-ulate your mission and serve those around you.

Take a Sample

Nehemiah did not need to inspect everyone or every part of the wall before beginning work. "Nehemiah did not circle the entire city, but only the southern portion, perhaps because he did not feel a need to see the whole wall in order to assess the job awaiting him."[1] Nehemiah inspected a portion of the wall. He reviewed a sample of the cracked wall. So should you. The workplace changes all the time. It is nearly impossible to assess the total need of your workplace and the people in it. Once you have completed a needs assessment of your current group of coworkers, a new colleague will have come aboard.

❖ Prayerfully consider an amount of time to inspect the need of your workplace. Some people may feel two weeks is enough time to see the true need of those around them, while others may take a month.

Look at your coworkers. Watch their actions and their work. Do you see behavior that dishonors our Lord? If so, ask yourself, "Why would my coworkers act this way?" Maybe the problem is your behavior toward them. Perhaps there is a problem at home or in some other relationship in their lives. Maybe the source of the pain causing their bizarre behavior is a need for Christ. In this inspection process you will find Christians and non-Christians with great needs. Be sensitive to believers and nonbelievers alike. Capturing your workplace for Christ requires that you minister to and serve other Christians as well as inviting non-Christians to feast at His banquet table.

Personal Relations

As you encounter your coworkers, note how they interact. Are they hostile and angry, or do they meet you and others warmly, extending a hand of friendship? Are your coworkers at ease, or do they seem tense and agitated? Do your coworkers smile, or do they exhibit the stress of a life yearning for something more? Look for the needs of your colleagues in the way they interact with you and others.

Written Correspondence

Look at the memos and letters your colleagues send. Do they fire off letters to set the record straight? Are they saying they need a taller chair when they really need a ladder to the Savior? Do your colleagues write memos expressing their disgust with someone or some policy when they really need someone or some policy to accept them? Look for the needs of your workplace by watching the tone and the words of written correspondence.

Quality of Work

Has the quality of your coworkers' output dropped? Has their error rate increased? Are they becoming increasingly isolated from their subordinates? Maybe their decreasing work performance tells you they need help! Perhaps the time has come to probe them for the cause of their pain.

Verbal Communication

Listen to the words and tone of your coworkers' expressions. Have they hung up the phone before saying good-bye? Do they unload on you and others the minute you say hello? Do your colleagues gossip about others? Their need is for your acceptance and forgiveness.

Disappointment

Listen to your associates for unfulfilled expectations. Maybe your coworkers accepted the positions at your place of employment with promises from your employer that have not been honored. Their pain and discouragement is real, and they need you to listen and understand. Perhaps some colleagues feel inadequate for the job at hand. They need your encouragement and the encouragement of our Savior. Listen for the heartfelt needs of your work force.

Life Changes

One of the greatest opportunities to transform your workplace for Christ is during transitions. Listen for transitions. Some are obvious. Perhaps your employer is laying off workers. Your colleagues can benefit from the knowledge that you rely on Christ to meet your needs. Maybe a new boss is coming on board. A kind word spoken to your new supervisor in favor of a coworker is a Christlike action.

Many transitions are hidden. Some of your coworkers are in a crisis at home. Their marriages may be breaking up, and they may be reluctant to discuss it at work. Perhaps a child is leaving the nest or a parent is dying. Whatever the transition, your coworker has a need for a friend and for Christ. You can offer both.

❖ As you inspect the cracks in the walls of your workplace, write your findings on your Rolodex cards. Now you have an organized system of identifying and praying for the needs of your coworkers.

Finding Needs Focuses the Message

In many companies employee theft is a big problem, yet there are other companies where employee theft does not exist. If you fail to stop and pray that God will reveal the needs of your workplace as you look and listen, your focus could become skewed. It would be easy to take a national statistic such as employee theft and assume it is a problem at your place of employment. But the easy way may lead you to miss the real needs in your workworld, causing the message of Christ you present to be less effective. Invest the time to evaluate the needs of your workplace. Two significant benefits will accrue to the process of capturing your workplace for Christ: the ability to motivate other Christians and an effective presentation of the gospel.

The Ability to Motivate Other Christians

Imagine yourself standing among a group of Christian coworkers. You voice a concern that employee theft is a big problem at your company. "Why, how do you know?" they ask. If your information comes from a publication about national trends, your meeting is over. If, however, you explain the evaluation process you completed and present the evidence you gathered, then you will find a group of believers motivated to help you capture your workplace for Christ.

"Then I said to them, 'You see the trouble we are in: Jerusalem lies in ruins, and its gates have been burned with fire. Come, let us rebuild the wall of Jerusalem, and we will no longer be in disgrace.' I also told them about the gracious hand of my God upon me and what the king had said to me. They replied, 'Let us start rebuilding.' So they began this good work" (Neh. 2:17–18).

How did Nehemiah motivate the people to work with him? He reported the facts of his evaluation of the cracked walls of Jerusalem and disclosed God's direction on the plan. How will you motivate other Christians to stand with you as you, together, transform your workplace for Christ? By reporting the results of your evaluation of your workplace's cracked walls. Your Christian coworkers will gain confidence from your evaluation and knowledge of God's direction of the plan.

Effective Presentation of the Gospel

Imagine you are looking for opportunities to share Christ with a needy coworker. If you fail to complete the needs evaluation and rely on someone else to conduct the research, your message may not be heard. For example, I read that absenteeism is a major problem in workplaces around the country. In an effort to expedite my passion to bring Christ into the workplace, I could have relied on that study to help focus my understanding of the needs around me. I may have engaged people in conversation about absenteeism, hoping that a door would open for me to share Christ. But if I had followed this easy course of action, my words would have fallen on deaf ears. Absenteeism was not a problem in our company, and I am sure my coworkers would have thought I was crazy to suggest it was a problem. Instead, I invested the time to stop, look, and listen long enough to uncover the true needs around me. Understanding those needs focused my message of Christ for maximum impact.

13

Evaluate Your Work Force
Step 3

My wife, Teri, loves to dig in the dirt. She enjoys gardening and planting and watching the fruit of her labor spring forth under the nourishment of the sun and the rain. Occasionally, she drags me out to help lift a heavy bag of dirt or to do some other task for which I am uniquely suited.

How I Learned about Soil

There is one spot in our front yard where grass will not grow no matter what we do. Each year Teri assures me, "The grass will grow there this year." Year after year we work that spot, but the grass still refuses to grow. So far we have not grown grass there, but we have learned a lot about soil.

Landscaping requires various layers of different types of soil to provide a base for sod. Fill dirt is the first layer. It is cheap, useful only as a filler. It won't support life because it has no organic components, but it holds things in place.

Planting soil is rich with nutrients and organic material that cause plants to grow. This type of dirt is valuable; from it sprouts beauty and life. Planting soil lays on top of the fill dirt. The sod is laid on top of the planting soil so the roots of the grass can work their way into the feast that awaits.

Sand is the third type of material used in the landscaping process. It is big and coarse and abrasive. Sand is spread over the sod and, like its fill dirt relative, holds the sod in place. When sand is first applied it is very visible, but as time passes so does the sand. Soon the abrasive sand is gone.

The Compost of Your Workplace

Our workplaces are a lot like soil. In any place of employment you will find a group of people with varied backgrounds, interests, and personalities—a sort of "human compost." They mix together within the confines of an office or factory. Personalities rub against each other, sometimes causing friction, other times causing friendship.

Our whole lives are spent bumping into people we hardly know and rarely take the time to know. We mix with others every day at work without really discovering who they are. Chapter 12 challenged us to evaluate the needs around us. In order to be aware of the needs of our coworkers, we must understand the condition of their hearts.

A good gardener knows the type of dirt he is working with. He knows the types of plants that flourish in certain kinds of dirt. The gardener knows how receptive his dirt will be to life. He knows when the dirt needs to be tilled and watered.

Like wise gardeners, we must know the soil that surrounds us. We must determine how receptive our colleagues will be to the message of life. Knowing the condition of their hearts will make our efforts effective and relevant.

We must plant the seed of Christ in our coworkers, then leave the outcome to them and God. We cannot control the decision of a coworker to follow or grow in Christ, but that does not lessen our responsibility to make Christ known. We must know the condition of their hearts so we can know their receptivity to His message.

Jesus' Parable of the Four Soils

Jesus' parable of the sower describes four kinds of soil, but it is really a story about the different ways people receive the gospel: "A farmer went out to sow his seed. As he was scattering the seed, some fell along the path, and the birds came and ate it up. Some fell on rocky places, where it did not have much soil. It sprang up quickly, because the soil was shallow. But when the sun came up, the plants were scorched, and they withered because they had no root. Other seed fell among thorns, which grew up and choked the plants. Still other seed fell on good soil, where it produced a crop—a hundred, sixty or thirty times what was sown. He who has ears, let him hear." (Matt. 13:1–9)

Hard Soil

The first type of soil Christ mentions is the hard ground on the path, which seemed impenetrable. The sower threw the seed, but the ground was so hard that it never took root. In fact, the soil was so hard that the seed found no place to reside and the birds easily picked it off the ground.

Because I have walked paths that were familiar to the soles of many shoes, I can imagine what the path in the story was like. It was hard packed, the result of hundreds and thousands of feet walking over it. An appearance of a glaze covered the dirt, rendering it impenetrable. Growth and life abounded on either side but not in the dirt on the path. It had been hardened over the years by the people that walked over it.

Some people are like hard soil. You know them. Like the path, these people have hearts that are hard. They may seem angry and irritated much of the time. Remember Mike's boss in chapter 10. He suffers from a hard heart. The hardening process occurred over many years and is the result of a past of painful trampling by the world. Planting a gospel seed with him and others like him seems to fall on deaf ears. "Been there, done that" is his response to any effort to enrich his life. He is experienced, and his experience has taught him that all this "Jesus stuff" is not what it is cracked up to be. You may drop a seed in his life, but he may ridicule you and pass your effort off as nonsense.

It is disconcerting to find someone's heart in this indifferent condition. "How do I reach him?" "Where do I go from here?" These are valid questions, but the first question I believe you should ask yourself is, "Is this person made in the image of God?" Since the answer is yes, the hard-hearted person is not a person to write off in your plan to capture your workplace for Christ. If you understand the condition of his heart, it will help you cope with the reaction you may get as you plant gospel seeds. Furthermore, you can relax, knowing it may take many months or years. You may never sense any response to the call of Christ in his life. Still, God wants you to include the hard hearted as you capture your workplace for Christ because, unchanged, their eternal home is with Satan. "When anyone hears the message about the kingdom and does not understand it, the evil one comes and snatches away what was sown in his heart" (Matt. 13:19). Hunker down for the long haul. You may be God's only messenger to your hard-hearted friend.

Rocky Soil

Jesus said the seed took root in the rocky soil and it "sprang up quickly, because the soil was shallow" (Matt. 13:5). These may be the walking wounded in your workplace. Perhaps they made a decision for Christ in an emotional moment. They may have identified themselves as Christians at one time but, due to sin, they do not believe they are Christians today. Maybe they responded to the compelling message of Christ but never left the baggage of past sin at the Cross, therefore, they still labor under a burden of guilt. These people are seeking something of substance from God.

Do you remember Jimmy and Kay from chapter 1? They were so desperate for something to fill the chasm of their souls that they turned to each other, forsaking the families they had created. Earlier in their lives, the gospel seed was planted, but it fell on rocky, shallow soil. Perhaps unconfessed sin kept them from a deeper understanding of who Christ is and His will for them. For whatever reason, their earlier commitment to Christ proved unfruitful, so Jimmy and Kay looked for love elsewhere.

Should you forget these coworkers as you develop your plan? Like their hard-hearted counterparts, they are made in the image of God. God loves them and desires a growing relationship with them. "What was sown on rocky places is the man who hears the word and at once receives it with joy. But since he has no root, he lasts only a short time. When trouble or persecution comes because of the word, he quickly falls away" (Matt. 13:20–21). Unless these shallow souls change, their fate is sealed along with the hardhearted. But be encouraged. These coworkers have some openness to your message.

They have probably experienced the warmth of Christ at some point in the past and long for it again. Maybe your encouragement will help them understand that Christ desires to forgive their past so they can press forward into the eternal future. Perhaps you are the only messenger of this good news they will encounter prior to standing in judgment before God.

Thorny Soil

Jonathan, who was mentioned in chapter 4, was like soil rich with thorns. This pastor was highly committed to his calling, but slowly the thorns of the world pricked his attention and damaged his ministry. That is typical of those stuck in thorny soil. They are distracted by the creature comforts of our age. Although sincere in their faith, they are torn by the rationalization that their earthly pursuit is somehow more noble than their call to serve Christ. Who among us has not been detained by the lure of the beautiful bloom that is attached to the thorns?

Jesus compares this condition of the heart to soil, but the soil itself is not the problem. The thorns that grow out of the soil create the difficulty. It may be rich soil, but the added distraction of the thorns causes the sprouting life to die.

You see these thorny sorts at work on Monday morning, and you very likely see them at church on Sunday morning too. They are followers of Christ, sincere in their intellectual belief, but distracted from the spiritual discipline that brings about growth. These Christians believe they can taste all that the world offers and grow in their faith as well. Christ, however, declares that mindset is false. "What was sown among the thorns is the man who hears the word, but the worries of this life and the deceitfulness of wealth choke it, making it unfruitful" (Matt. 13:22).

Your calling to transform your workplace for Christ may be specifically to reach your thorny brothers and sisters in Christ. This group should have the most knowledge of the Word of the three groups we have discussed. During transitions such as divorce or a job-related crisis, these thorny Christians sometimes see the deceitfulness of the world and draw closer to Christ. You can help prune the thorns from their path and help them locate the good soil of Christ.

If these believers do not find a friend such as you, they may never again enjoy a growing, life-giving relationship with Christ. Be a good gardener for Christ and lead the thorny to restoration in Christ.

Good Soil

You have met many good-soil Christians in the pages of this book. Kathy Montgomery, Brian Willett, Darlene Mullen, Jane Folk, Bill and Millie Morgan, Judge Guthrey, Truett Cathy, David Dorsey, and Guy Doud are a few of those whose feet are firmly planted in the soil of the Savior. These are uncompromising Christians. Faith in Christ sets their agenda, and from the activity of their lives springs much fruit for our Lord. "But what was sown on good soil is the man who hears the word and understands it. He produces a crop, yielding a hundred, sixty or thirty times what was sown" (Matt. 13:23).

Every day these good-soil Christians model the ten virtues every workplace needs: love, encouragement, forgiveness, accountability, balanced living, excellence, communication, keeping promises, stewardship, and integrity. These people lead the way for Christ, not by commanding but by humbly serving in His name. These sincere and focused Christians are not perfect, but they understand the grace that Christ has given them. Because of their thankfulness to Him and their ever deepening relationship with Him, they share Christ with others. These people step out in faith and capture their workplaces for Christ.

❖ Examine yourself. Are you like the hard soil, rocky soil, thorny soil, or the good soil? God is working with you, and He desires for you to enjoy the relationship that comes from dwelling in the good soil. Begin praying that God will show you the areas of your life that need adjustment. Begin to read His Word daily.

❖ Ask God to show you the condition of your coworkers' hearts. If you ask, He will prompt you to be sensitive to your coworkers, and He will reveal what He wants you to know. God is the Judge, not you or me. Allow God to give you insight into the hearts of your coworkers so you can be more effective for Him.

Why Must You Evaluate Your Work Force?

Step 3 (evaluating your work force) is not an invitation to take God's checklist and grade your coworkers. This is not an exercise to arrange them in a Christlike pecking order, with you at the top of the list. Step 3 requires you to prayerfully and purposely pay closer attention to your colleagues and, under the direction of the Holy Spirit, see them in greater depth. You must evaluate your work force so you can serve them better, pray specifically for them, and begin determining who might join you in your effort to transform your workplace for Christ.

You can serve your colleagues better if you understand them more. From the assessment of their hearts you can refine your message to be relevant to their lives. You can tailor your approach to meet them where they are.

You can pray more effectively for your coworkers if you know their hearts. You can ask God to break through the hard soil, add depth to the rocky soil, convict the thorny soil, or encourage the good soil. Specific prayer is effective, and the condition of a coworker's heart is an appropriate reason to pray.

You can add to your ranks if you take the time to know the hearts of those around you. The effort to capture a workplace for Christ is blessed if only one person is involved, but God honors "two or more" at work for Him, especially when the task is capturing your workplace for Him. Knowing the hearts of those around you opens the door to invite others to share in the joy of the journey.

14

Marshal Your Resources
Step 4

Randy Hughes left the Portland Promise Keepers meeting bent on capturing his world for Christ. That included his workplace. On Sunday, Randy spoke to his Sunday school class about God's movement in his life. Using the blackboard, Randy wrote the key words of the points he was making. He brought a video of his experience and shared it. That afternoon in the family playroom, Randy told his wife and kids what God was doing in his life. Using the setting of the playroom, Randy told them that he realized he had been playing with God until this encounter. Now he was going to get serious about leading the family to a deeper faith.

Monday morning, Randy arrived at work with an even stronger desire to transform his workplace for Christ. At first he thought about simply walking up to coworkers and sharing his faith; however, he realized that approach might not be effective. Randy thought, *Is there a tool I can use to take action for Christ?* For several days, Randy pondered this question. Gradually the demands of his work grew, pushing his desire to bring Christ with him to work farther and farther down the list of things to do.

Recognize Your Resources

Once there was a great flood in the West. The water was standing about three feet deep when an emergency worker showed up at

Sandy's house saying, "We are evacuating the area. Come on and go with us in the truck." Sandy replied, "Go ahead. God is going to deliver me from this flood." The emergency worker moved to the next home. A few hours later, the water was about chest deep. A friend from down the lane showed up in his fishing boat asking, "Sandy, want to get out with us?" Sandy answered, "No, God is going to deliver me!" Still later the water reached the ceiling in Sandy's home and she was standing on the roof. A helicopter hovered overhead and a man leaned out and said, "Hang on, we are going to drop a ladder. Grab it and climb up." But Sandy said, "Move on. God is going to deliver me." The helicopter flew away. It wasn't long before the swiftly flowing water carried Sandy and her house away and Sandy was killed.

When Sandy met God she said, "I depended on You to deliver me from the flood. Why didn't You?" God replied, "Do you remember that emergency worker in a truck?" "Yes," replied Sandy. God said, "Well, I sent her to deliver you. Do you remember your friends in the boat?" "Sure, I do," answered Sandy. God replied, "I sent them to deliver you. How about the helicopter, remember that?" Sandy nodded and said, "I guess you sent them too." God instructed, "I tried to deliver you at least three times, but you did not see that I would use a human means to deliver you."

This familiar story illustrates a great truth. Many of us are like Randy. We want to capture our workplace for Christ, but we think the cards are stacked against us. We often feel the need for some additional "spiritual" tool to communicate the message of Christ. So we wait to capture our companies for Christ, expecting God to send an angel or some new method. We may, like Sandy, look back and see that God had given us the tools all along.

We live in a great age—the information age, the communication age. Today we have more ways to communicate than ever before. It is an exciting time. Have you considered all the tools at your disposal? Do you realize the variety of resources that exist today to communicate the message of Christ to your coworkers? Don't become paralyzed like Randy, wondering what to do. Take an inventory of your toolbox. Realize that God may have already given you resources that although secular can still be used for His glory. Tools man may intend for efficiency or financial gain or human success, God can use to build His kingdom and earthly civilization.

Tools for the Task

Look around your workplace for the tools you need for the task. They are everywhere. Ask God to show you how to creatively use them for His glory. Here are a few of the tools I see; maybe you can add others.

E-mail

Most workplaces today have an E-mail system. Though there are a number of different systems in use, all of them operate to facilitate communication. An E-mail system is great for breaking the ice when capturing your workplace for Christ. You must have a screen name to use E-mail. Why not choose one that reflects your faith? For example, "Faith," "Heart4God," "Gracegiver," "Forgiven," "Eph428," "John316," and "Godluvsu" are possible screen names. Imagine the questions you will get using one of these names. Once the questions are asked, you are free to capture your workplace for Christ.

Does your E-mail system have a mailbox component? You can post a Scripture in your mailbox and others can retrieve it. Maybe you would like to write a thought for the day. Your coworkers can visit your mailbox and be inspired.

Web Page

The Internet facilitates communication around the world. I send messages to a friend in Korea via the Internet free of charge. Incredible! Closer to home you can create a web page that your coworkers, customers, and vendors can visit. The page could include your testimony, a calendar of upcoming events in your church, a Scripture and thought for the day, and inspiring stories about other Christians.

Screen Savers

Screen savers keep images from burning into the computer screen. That happens if the screen is inactive for a short period of time. You can protect your screen and burn a message for Christ into the hearts of coworkers by creatively using your screen saver. Most screen saver programs give you the option to post a message that rapidly scrolls across the screen. Post a message of Scripture. When your coworkers come into your work area, they will read the message–Scripture. You can also post a message as simple as "God Loves You."

I have Psalm 118:24 posted on my screen saver. Many coworkers ask, especially on the tough days, "How can you rejoice today?" That is an open door to share Christ in a non-threatening way.

Bulletin Boards

It seems anticlimactic to mention the traditional bulletin board after discussing the high tech opportunities around us. Still, most break rooms have a bulletin board where employees can post information of interest to coworkers—cars for sale, kittens for free, piano lessons, etc. Why not post a Christ-honoring message? You might use a message like those discussed above or even a provocative sign such as "For Spiritual Help call 555-1234" (using your phone number, of course). Maybe this anonymous announcement will intersect with someone in need. Take posters from your church and put them up. Tag the poster with, "For more information, call Joe Smith at 555-1234."

Company Newsletters

Your workplace may distribute a newsletter to its employees. Ask if you can provide an inspirational article. Then write an article yourself or ask your pastor to write one. Perhaps you have a favorite poem or verse of Scripture. Be sure the line, "This article was provided by Joe Smith" appears. You are not trying to gain popularity, but you are trying to make your faith in God known to your coworkers in a non-threatening way.

Company Meetings

Ben McDavid's employer holds lunch meetings for all employees on a regular basis. A blessing was not being offered before the meal, so Ben asked his boss, who is of another faith, if he could pray before the meal. Ben's boss agreed and now Ben is capturing his workplace for Christ. The response by his coworkers to a simple prayer before the meal has been overwhelming. Your workplace probably holds regular meetings too. Could you offer a blessing before a meal? Maybe a meal is not served at your meeting. What is wrong with starting the meeting with a prayer? Think of other ways you can use your company meetings to capture your workplace for Christ.

Break Rooms

Break rooms are gathering places. You can utilize bulletin boards as was mentioned earlier. Does your break room have a television? Lay out the program guide for the Christian channel in your area. Tune your break room television in to that channel. Place pamphlets outlining the plan of salvation on tables.

Break Time

Most of us look forward to our breaks during the day to go and rest. Take advantage of this time to recharge your batteries. Find a quiet spot in the break room and take a few minutes to complete a devotion. Not only will this be meaningful to you, others may follow your example.

You can also use your break for relationship building. Invite coworkers to share the time. Get to know them. Sample the soil of their soul. Check on those who have experienced a transition in life due to death, divorce, birth of a child, etc. Inquire after any who have asked you to hold them accountable. Lead a small group Bible study.

Your Product

Your work is a resource that can be used to capture your workplace for Christ. If your work product is shabby, your witness will be impaired. If your work is excellent, coworkers will be interested in what you have to say. Begin to see your work as an act of worship to God. Your coworkers will notice.

I have mentioned many tools that are common to most workplaces, but other tools for the task exist. Many are unique to a workplace setting. Take action now.

❖   Make a list of the tools mentioned above.
❖   Look around your workplace for other tools that can be used
     to capture your workplace for Christ. Add them to the list.
❖   Beside each entry, list at least one way that tool can be cre-
     atively used for the Kingdom.

Hired Help for the Task

There is a sea of resources outside your workplace available to help
capture your workplace for Christ. Here are a few impacting
resources that you can bring to your workplace.

Character Works

     "Character Works" is an employee character-building program
centered in the life of Christ. While the tone of this program is not
overly religious, it is provocative. This program has been accepted
for use by governmental agencies, hospitals, automotive service
providers, financial service companies, and many more.
     The program leads the employee through an introspective look
at the kind of character he or she may exhibit versus the kind of
character he or she needs. Ten Christlike character traits are used to
provoke the employee to seek deeper meaning in life. *Character Works*
uses a workbook and is maintained through a monthly publication
known as *Messages from the Principles*. Employers have seen people
come to know and grow in Christ. (For more information about
"Character Works" contact Faith at Work, Inc., P.O. Box 11328,
Montgomery, AL 36111 or call 800-383-2653.)

Out of Their Faces and into Their Shoes

     You may not feel comfortable sharing your faith with another
person. John Kramp's book *Out of Their Faces and into Their Shoes*, is
tailor-made for you.[1] Learn how to naturally share your faith in
Christ with love and compassion. This study of "lostology" is fun and
enlightening.

Seeking Solid Ground

     Most of us are seeking solid ground. Dr. John Trent in his book

Seeking Solid Ground insightfully leads us through Psalm 15 and the definition of godly character.[2] Do some of your coworkers show you disrespect? Maybe without even knowing it you have exhibited some character flaws. Check Trent's book and consider your character.

David, Man of Character
Dr. Gene Getz in his book *David* ("Men of Character" series) offers a beautiful description of godly character as seen in the life of David.[3]

The Grace Awakening
Do you get angry often? Are you suspicious of your coworkers? You need an awakening, a grace awakening. Dr. Chuck Swindoll teaches the grace of Christ in his book *The Grace Awakening*.[4]

LifeMapping
Maybe you have anger from past experiences that is keeping you from being effective for Christ. Dr. John Trent's book *LifeMapping* takes you through a step-by-step process to overcome your past and position yourself for a future in Christ.[5]

Can Man Live without God?
Dr. Ravi Zacharias answers this life-changing question in the book *Can Man Live without God?*[6] This book is a compilation of lectures Zacharias gave at Harvard University.

Jesus Works Here
Robert Tamasy edited this book of articles on subjects ranging from time management to decision making to getting fired. All of these subjects are important if you are serious about capturing your workplace for Christ and acknowledging *Jesus Works Here*.[7]

The "Faith at Work" Television Series
This series consists of twelve thirty-minute segments that highlight actual workplace stories of people who have successfully integrated their faith into their work. The program includes a workbook and can be viewed on an individual or group basis. It is available for purchase or rental through Faith at Work, Inc. (For

more information on this series, contact Faith at Work, Inc., P.O. Box 11328, Montgomery, AL 36111 or call 800-383-2653.)

Young Business Leaders

This dynamic organization reaches out to men in the workplace organizing banquets, small group Bible studies, and retreats. Contact them at 2420 Arlington Avenue, Birmingham, AL 35205 or call 205-933-0090.

Christian Medical Ministry

This organization ministers to the unique needs of medical school students and physicians. Contact them at 2420 Arlington Ave, Birmingham, AL 35205 or call 205-933-0304.

Christian Business Men's Committee

This ministry develops men and women in the business community to carry out the Great Commission. Contact them at P.O. Box 3308, Chattanooga, TN 37404 or call 800-566-CBMC.

Fellowship of Companies for Christ

This ministry equips and encourages chief executives and company owners to operate their businesses and conduct their personal lives according to biblical principles in pursuit of Christ's eternal objectives. Contact them at 4201 N. Peachtree Road, Atlanta, GA 30341 or call 770-457-9700.

We serve a God of the everyday. He equips us with tools to use for the task He has given us. Sometimes we overlook the obvious, everyday kind of resource that could be used to build His kingdom. Be creative and take a fresh look at the everyday resources around you!

15

Take Your Stand
Step 5

When the Lord took hold of Charles Jemison, He tamed a tiger. Jemison is a supervisor for a manufacturing firm. He had accepted Christ at an early age. The demanding work schedule of the aggressive Jemison preempted church attendance. As he progressed in his position, Charles's schedule became more demanding. Thus fellowship and worship with other believers was limited. As the company he worked with grew, weekend work took priority, and Charles was rarely seen at the church he and his family attended.

Jemison and his family knew his work would be demanding and time consuming, but they believed his weekend work schedule would eventually lighten up. After a few months, however, nothing had changed, and he had grown comfortable devoting every day of the week to work.

What began as a short-term endurance race now was the pattern of his life. Charles quit going to church, and soon his personal time of prayer and Bible study ended as well. Charles was an accident waiting to happen.

A Bend in the Road

One Tuesday morning, Jemison received an urgent call informing him that a coworker had filed a complaint against him alleging sexual harassment. The months ahead were filled with depositions

191

and conferences with his attorneys. Charles was slipping away emo-
tionally. The possibility that the details of this case would become
public caused him to face the fact that his career was in jeopardy.
Charles fell deeper and deeper into an emotional pit. He hit his low
point in life.

Fortunately, he was married to a godly woman. She knew that
only God could bring her husband back, and she led him to begin
reading the Psalms. Jemison found himself under the care of the
Great Physician. His hunger for God's Word became insatiable. As
he moved beyond Psalms to other books of the Bible, God actively
taught the stubborn supervisor Who was in control. Jemison embarked
on a new pattern of prayer, study, personal, and corporate worship.
God lifted Charles out of the depths of his despair to an intimate
relationship with Him.

Traveling a New Road

Charles Jemison was back! Renewed and regenerated, Jemison
bounded into his office at the manufacturing plant with a refreshed
zeal for living and an obvious commitment to his Lord. He started
attending church with his family. He even began to financially support a South American missionary.

Each month Charles instructed his secretary to write a check
directly to the missionary. Jemison spoke openly with his coworkers
about the events at his church and how he would like to offer even
more assistance to God's man south of the border. Jemison was
indeed a changed man, but not a perfect man.

He looked up to missionaries as dedicated people who take the
gospel overseas to foreign lands, but he never thought about how
many of his coworkers needed Jesus.

It took the possibility of a ruined career to bring Jemison back
to God. It took a tragedy for him to see the mission field on which
he was standing, his workplace. Shay was one of the production line
employees who worked with Jemison. One morning she did not
report to work. This was unusual because Shay was always punctual.
Soon the news of her fatal accident on the way to work swept the
plant.

Jemison and his staff were devastated. "You cannot work this closely with someone and not feel the enormous impact of the loss," he told the staff. He continued speaking in an effort to comfort his coworkers, "While we will miss Shay now, we will see her in heaven." A hush fell over the room as Charles spoke those words. Tears flooded the eyes of those who really knew Shay. Sensing an increasing intensity of grief among his associates, Jemison offered these words, "In a tough time like this we must trust in the Scriptures, which assure us that when believers in Jesus Christ die, they will be with Him in glory!" A voice wavering under the emotional impact of the news spoke up and stopped Jemison cold: "That is just the problem, Mr. Jemison. Shay was not a Christian." Shay had heard all the reports of the activity of Jemison and his church. She knew Jemison was committed to his cause, but she had never been confronted with the message of Jesus Christ. Shay never understood that Christianity is not a cause but an eternal relationship with our Maker.

On the Right Road?

Now Jemison asked himself, "Why didn't I share Christ with Shay directly?" Shay was a good and moral person. It is easy to understand how Charles may have assumed she was a Christian. But being good and being moral by themselves will not buy you a ticket to eternal life with the Creator.

It is also possible that Jemison thought he had shared Christ with Shay and the others in his office when he told them about his church's activities. Maybe the now sorrowful supervisor assumed Shay would find Christ through the knowledge that her boss supported a South American missionary. Jemison may have sincerely thought that Shay would catch his faith and be saved.

But Jesus is clear on that point: "I am the way and the truth and the life. No one comes to the Father except through me" (John 14:6). Shay could not come to the Lord through Charles Jemison, only through our Savior, Jesus Christ. Our coworkers will not come to Christ simply because we live good and moral lives and talk about our faith-related activities. Our faith is not a cause that people catch, it is the truth intended to confront and convict.

Maybe Jemison knew what he was doing. Maybe he made a conscious decision not to evangelize his coworkers. Many Christians today suffer from the misguided belief that it is inappropriate to confront others in the workplace with the truth of Jesus Christ. If you think like this, ask yourself, "Is it appropriate that persons spend eternity in hell?" Peter wrote of our Lord, "He is patient with you, not wanting anyone to perish, but everyone to come to repentance" (2 Pet. 3:9).

"Not at work," you say. "I will share the gospel with my coworkers somewhere else." Where and when will you share your Lord with the needful from the office? The odds are that you never see most of your coworkers during nonworking hours. So when and where are you going to share the gospel with them? If you don't get around to it, who will? Charles Jemison may have used this argument and rationalized his way out of confronting his coworkers. Shay, his colleague, paid the eternal price for Charles's decision to defer sharing the convicting truth of God.

Another explanation for Jemison's inaction is probably the most dangerous. He may have wanted to reflect on the possibility of presenting Christ to his office. Jemison may have felt the subject required more study. Maybe he was simply unsure of his ability to share his faith. Jemison may have been lingering in the sin of indecision.

Indecision is a trap that catches us from time to time. It sounds acceptable to say we are studying the subject or that we are in training. Others applaud us for our interest in learning how we can do more for our Lord. A certain amount of study and training is helpful and needed, but too often the warmth of the study and training environment holds us back from actually entering the arena. Let's be honest; we frequently find that more study and training are needed because the coziness of our world is much less intimidating than the reality of taking the point for Christ into a real world situation, especially a workworld situation.

Indecision is very dangerous because it hides behind acceptable concerns and true needs. We need study and training in evangelism, but the finest training is a waste of time if we don't use it. Study and train, and then act decisively.

Share Christ Where You Are

Jesus did not command us to wait and develop a theory. He told us to "go and make disciples" (Matt. 28:19). Maybe you are an active missionary in your community. Your church may sponsor a soup kitchen or a clothes closet. I hope you are a part of those efforts. You may give money to help in those activities. If so, you are providing a necessary resource, and you are a vital member of the missions team. You are acting decisively in your community missions.

Most of our mission efforts are directed toward those who appear different from us. The housing project on the other side of town, the homeless living under a downtown bridge, and under-privileged children are favorite targets of our mission-related endeavors. All of these groups are worthy of hearing the gospel of Christ, and I strongly support any effort to evangelize them.

My challenge to you, however, is to add another venue to your mission mindset—your workplace. There you will find people that look very much like you look. In your workplace, most of your coworkers are in your economic class. You probably have similar needs and life situations. But do not let appearances lull you into an assumption that you and your coworkers share a common belief in Jesus Christ.

I ask you to make a Christ-honoring judgment about your coworkers based on their hearts and not their outward appearances. Jesus spoke to our tendency to make incorrect judgments when He told a crowd, "Stop judging by mere appearances, and make a right judgment" (John 7:24). We should evangelize persons based on their need for Christ, not on what we believe based solely on their appearance. Appearances can be deceiving—just ask Charles Jemison.

I also call you to take your stand because I believe God is calling a multitude of Christians in the marketplace to rise up and be counted for Him. Some may ask, "Is it appropriate to discuss Christ at work?" God gave you work for the purpose of building His kingdom and a civilization that honors Him. God created work. He owns it. My question is, why is it not appropriate to discuss Christ at work? The philosophy driving capturing your workplace for Christ is that you must demonstrate your love for Christ in and through your work before your words will be heard. Decisive Christ-honoring action is needed. You are God's envoy in your place of employment.

Shay's life has been lost for all eternity. Jemison could have shared the message of Christ with Shay, but he didn't. What will be said of you? As you look in the eyes of your coworkers today, ask yourself this question, "Am I absolutely certain that this colleague is bound for eternity with Jesus Christ?" If your answer to this question for just one of your coworkers is no, then you need to get serious about transforming your workplace for Christ!

Plan Your Action and Act on Your Plan

A defining moment in your walk with God has come. You have spent time with the Father in prayer. He is changing you. You have seen the needs of the others in your workplace. You have assessed your coworkers receptivity to the gospel, and you have taken an inventory of all the possible resources that could help you transform your workplace for Christ. A moment of decision has come, and your response to this activity of God in your life will determine what you truly believe about Him.

Action Point 1: Assemble the Team

You must call together those you assessed as the most dedicated to the ways of God. Meet them for lunch or on break or after work hours. Share with them the message God has laid on your heart. Invite them to join you and God on this exciting adventure.

You will find that some of these good-soil Christians have been laboring under the same burden. These encounters with your like-minded associates will be joyous as they confirm God's intent to establish Himself in all areas of our lives.

You may only find one other Christian in your place of employment willing to step out with you and claim the eight-to-five world for God. Praise God that He brought you and your friend together. If a larger number of believers assemble, then praise God even more. But remember, we serve the almighty, all-powerful Creator. He can accomplish His purpose if one or two or twenty of us yield our availability to Him.

Confer with other dedicated believers who are not a part of your work force. Ask them to pray with you as you step onto God's holy ground. I have found incredible support from my friends who have committed to pray for me. I am astonished at the God-given and divinely timed insight.

Action Point 2: Give Your Group a Name

Marketing professionals say that an organization's name is its best marketing tool. Give your group of believers a name. "Salt and Light" and "Action: All Christians Together in One Name" are two names of groups that exist in the workplace. This point of identity in the workplace will cause others to ask the purpose of your group. What a witness opportunity!

Action Point 3: Establish a Regular Meeting

Begin to meet as a group on a regular basis. You may have discovered a meeting room at your office that could be made available for the meeting. Establish a time and a place for the meeting and do not cancel it, even if only one of you can attend on a given day. That one member of the team needs to meet with God and pray for the others.

Undergird everything you do with prayer. Call on God without ceasing. The first meetings should be devoted solely to prayer. Pray for each other and your families. Pray for wisdom to clearly discern His will in your lives. Pray for unity among your group but diversity among your abilities and opportunities. Pray that God will soften your hearts to the enormous needs that abound in your workplace. Pray that each of you will be bold in carrying the banner of the Lord. Pray that any obstacles to your presentation of Christ will be knocked down. Pray for the needs of specific members of your work team and that God will show you how to respond in a salty way. Confess your sin, and ask Christ to forgive you. Celebrate all He has done and is doing for you.

As you collectively and earnestly seek the Lord, He will begin to change each member of your group and reveal His direction for your corporate efforts. He will direct you to opportunities to plant the gospel seed. When members of the team begin sharing what God is doing in their lives, your group will need to take more time for meetings.

An uncommon unity should emerge among the members of the group regarding the plan to capture your workplace for Christ. You have prayed for such unity in the same way Paul prayed for the Christians in Rome: "May the God who gives endurance and encouragement give you a spirit of unity among yourselves as you follow Christ Jesus, so that with one heart and mouth you may glorify the God and Father of our Lord Jesus Christ" (Rom. 15:5–6). This Christlike unity affirms the direction of God in your efforts.

During the meetings, discuss ways you and the others can use your unique gifts to respond to the challenge at hand. The formation of a band of believers at your place of employment is no accident. God has appointed you to work together, and He has given each member of the team special abilities to carry out His purpose. Your spiritual giftedness is important to the specific plan of action that is discussed below.

Action Point 4: Develop a Written Plan

In these early stages of the group's development, it is essential to commit God's direction to writing. This hard copy of God's plan is valuable for at least three reasons.

❖ The process of producing the document will help hone your group's thoughts and feelings into a cohesive, workable plan. Any effort or activity you attempt will be better if you take the time to write it down.

❖ The process of writing your plan will help build unity among the team. This is an activity requiring broad participation. Everyone's voice should be heard. Everyone should feel that their input is worthy. Everyone should feel a part of the team.

❖ The written explanation of your mission will guide your group as your ministry progresses. As time passes we often find ourselves trying to accomplish tasks and complete activities that have little in common with our central purpose. This written statement of purpose and plan helps keep you on track as you move into the future.

I suggest your document be divided into three sections: mission statement, program, and evaluation.

Mission Statement. The Mission Statement is a concise phrase, sentence, or paragraph describing your purpose for existing individually or as a group. This statement will help you make decisions. I have seen simple, straightforward mission statements such as "To honor God" and "To know God and to make Him known." I have also seen more elaborate mission statements such as "Following the leadership of our Lord and Savior, we will be intentional witnesses for Him to our fellow employees."

The mission statement guides your activities. For instance, suppose you and your band of believers are approached about participating in the company picnic. Your first step is to filter that request through your mission statement. Assuming your specific mission statement is consistent with those presented above, I believe you would choose to participate in the picnic. Other invitations of participation, however, may not be acceptable. For instance, your company may plan "Casino Night" as an extracurricular activity. Your mission statement helps you ensure consistent decisions.

Your activity should be consistent with your mission statement. You may decide to participate in the picnic by offering to be responsible for the cleanup. This thankless job reveals your servant heart, and the fact that you intend to leave the picnic area cleaner than when you arrived shows your coworkers a genuine commitment to excellence.

Program. Much of the activity that will comprise your program can be planned in advance. Often situations will present themselves on the spur of the moment. You must be nimble and respond quickly. This is another reason you need a written plan. With the written plan in hand, each member of your group will be able to decide if an activity is suitable. The plan should improve your response time.

I suggest you create a monthly calendar as part of your plan. Look for specific events and target those events for participation. For example, your institution may support the March of Dimes. In many cities this charity holds a walkathon or some similar event to raise money. Plan in advance to challenge the rest of your company to participate and raise funds.

Your company may offer a Christmas luncheon for its employees. Volunteer now to help serve the meal. Take responsibility for sharing Christ in creative ways during the uniquely Christian holiday seasons of Christmas and Easter, which are becoming increasingly secularized.

You should plan speakers for your regular meetings. A member of your group may wish to give a testimony. Someone in the community may have a program of particular interest. A local pastor may come in to encourage you.

Don't forget to combine training with action. *Evangelism Explosion* or *Christian Witness Training* (CWT) are both excellent programs. The topics of dealing with adversity and dealing with difficult people are ideal for your group. Effective communication may be another idea for training. There are many Bible study guides that would be great for group sessions. Plan your calendar for a full twelve months to include events, speakers, and training.

Evaluation. Your group must evaluate its work if it is to continue. As soon as is practical after an event, prayerfully consider how the event and your participation could have been an even greater witness for our Lord. Record your responses and file them. The next year, refer to the evaluation for planning purposes.

Action Point 5: Act on Your Plan

I once saw a quote that read, "Begin somewhere; you cannot build a reputation on what you intend to do." Let me rephrase this in the context of our mission: "Begin somewhere; you cannot honor God with what you intend to do."

James said, What good is it, my brothers, if a man claims to have faith but has no deeds? Can such faith save him? Suppose a brother or sister is without clothes and daily food. If one of you says to him, 'Go, I wish you well; keep warm and well fed,' but does nothing about his physical needs, what good is it? In the same way, faith by itself, if it is not accompanied by action, is dead. But someone will say, 'You have faith; I have deeds.' Show me your faith without deeds, and I will show you my faith by what I do. You believe that there is one God. Good! Even the demons believe that—and shudder. (James 2:14–19)

James is saying that the evidence of our faith is our work. Our faith manifests itself through our deeds. You have prayed and planned. Your heart is solidly fixed on the Savior. Even the demons believe there is one God and know the Scriptures. So what is different about you? Christlike action sets you apart. Now is the time to act.

Invite others to join your group. Ultimately, your aim is to increase the kingdom of God. Your team is a part of the Kingdom, so increasing your numbers means Kingdom growth.

Ask the persons responsible for a company meal if you can ask a blessing before the meal. A friend of mine asked his Jewish boss if he could ask a blessing before a meal. He was given permission, and the response was so overwhelmingly positive that my friend is now asked to say a blessing before all meals served at his office.

Post announcements in your breakroom of upcoming events in the community where Christ will be honored. List your name and number for further information. Distribute tracts in the breakroom and other common areas with your name or the name of your group listed for more information.

Finally, make yourself accountable to another believer for implementing your plan. Share your actions with one another, encouraging each other to be bolder and more creative. God will honor your courageous deeds resulting from your faith.

A Probing Auditor's Discovery

Bailey Anthony is a staff auditor for one of the world's largest financial institutions, working out of one of the firm's regional offices. Some years ago Bailey felt a burden to bring Christ to her company—no small task for this staff auditor.

She saw the needs of her coworkers. Her first step of action was to fall on her knees. From that humble position Bailey allowed God to change her and give her the courage to inquire about the possibility of organizing a Bible study. Her company had allowed a gay and lesbian group to form, but to Bailey's astonishment the institution refused to allow a group of Christians to assemble in their workplace.

Bailey didn't pick up her belongings and find employment elsewhere. For the next two years she prayed daily that God would soften the hearts of the decision makers and allow the formation of her group. During those two years Bailey stepped out on God's turf and invited other Christians at her place of employment to join her and God in this task. To her amazement, she found that a few of the others shared her burden. God was working!

The group began praying daily that God would open a door for them to become intentional and welcomed in their efforts. One day a booklet arrived at her desk entitled "The Diversity Concept Booklet." This booklet described her employer's tolerance of a wide range of views and lifestyles and the process necessary for employees to organize "support groups." Bailey gazed at the booklet as she heard the Lord say, "Here is your open door. Why are you sitting there?"

The management team responsible for implementing the diversity program had not anticipated that a group of Christians would seek to organize and become known within the company. It took the decision makers several weeks to respond to Bailey's request. Then one day she received an E-mail: "Your support group has been approved." The news spread quickly among the believers who had been praying with Bailey. They were elated and immediately began to organize.

Finally, Christians could come out of the closet. Soon other groups formed in the company's regional offices. They meet regularly to discuss problems, pray for each other, study the Bible, and hear speakers.

Today at Bailey's workplace a Scripture verse and meditation thought is broadcast over the E-mail system. What a creative Kingdom-building use of the resources of the largest financial institution in the world.

Bailey Anthony is not a member of the management team at her place of employment. She does not have broad decision-making authority. But she made a decision to follow God's will in her life, and today thousands of lost souls will be presented the gospel of Jesus Christ.

The Manager on a Mission

The executive vice president of a large banking company felt God urging him to transform his workplace for Christ. His company already enjoyed the Thursday morning visit of a local pastor who offered a devotional thought and prayer. These Thursday morning meetings had become a weekly highlight for many employees.

As time passed, this senior manager wanted to take his employees deeper. He wanted to see persons come to know Christ personally. This boss witnessed divorces, addictions, abuse, and other serious consequences of sin. He also found pettiness, jealousy, and anger in his workforce. The EVP saw the problems, and he knew that Christ was the answer.

He began to pray that God would show him how to honor his Creator in the workplace. With an insight as clear as if he had been studying for weeks, this manager developed a program to teach Christlike values to his employees. A workbook was distributed to all employees, and a seminar was held during working hours. Spinning off of the workbook program was a weekly Bible study for interested employees. This group met for lunch on Wednesdays.

The presentation and the workbook were not overtly Christian, but the material was written and presented in a salty way that caused those seeking God to ask, "Where did this stuff come from?" Bingo! Evangelism time! Lives were changed forever. Nonbelievers from a variety of backgrounds and life circumstances came to know the Lord. Backslidden Christians were encouraged to take hold of God's lifeline. Needs of all types were met.

That executive vice president is me. I have been humbled to see God work in our place of employment. God used this experience to teach me the real burden of management. Members of the management team are stewards of the time, talent, and future of those we serve, our employees. The manner in which managers who are Christian choose to respond to this unique opportunity reveals what they believe about God.

The Commencement

Those who finish high school or college usually hear a commencement address. The message is typically the same: "Hardworking souls who complete a study are just beginning. To finish is to commence." So it is with you.

You have the tools to begin an intentional effort to bring your nonbelieving coworkers to Christ and build up the Christians around you. How are you going to respond?

Undecided? Please understand this truth. If your business or institution fails today, that event will not shut down the kingdom of God. But if you fail to invite God into your business or institution, then many of your coworkers will be shut out of the kingdom of God.

Charles Jemison's life teaches us two important lessons. First, God uses our work to mold us in His image. Second, we must invite God into our workplaces so He can mold the lives of our coworkers. A needy world of workers awaits your action.

The following actions may help you as you take your stand for Christ:

❖ Discuss your journey that has led you to desire to transform your workplace for Christ.

❖ Read John 14:6 and Matthew 28:19–20. What do your actions toward your coworkers reveal about your obedience to the claim of Christ in John 14:6 and His command in Matthew 28:19–20?

❖ Have you looked beyond your coworkers' good and moral lives to see their need for Christ? If not, do you believe Christ's claim in John 14:6 is true?

❖ Do you believe faith in Christ can be caught by others if you never say a word to them about Jesus?

❖ Do you believe it is inappropriate to share the gospel at work? If so, what scriptural basis justifies your position?

❖ Reread the four action points discussed in this chapter. Commit to God and your accountability group to begin the process of capturing your workplace for Christ. Agree to discuss your actions each week. Covenant to hold each other accountable. Draft a written contract to be signed by all parties.

❖ Now ask Him to remove any obstacles that exist within you. Ask God to prepare the hearts of those He desires to join you in this eternal work. Pray that the needs of your coworkers will be clear to you and that you will proceed boldly to transform your workplace for Christ.

Conclusion

Helen Keller said, "The only thing worse than being blind is to have sight but no vision." I hope you do not suffer from such blindness. You have studied the Christlike principles of love, encouragement, forgiveness, balanced living, accountability, excellence, communication, keeping promises, stewardship, and integrity. I hope you have captured a vision of how you can bring those qualities to your workplace and have fashioned that vision into a written plan of action.

The Prophet and His Vision

You may be asking yourself, "Is this vision to capture my workplace for Christ realistic? Will my effort have any effect at all?" Solomon said, "Where there is no vision, the people are unrestrained, but happy is he who keeps the law" (Prov. 29:18, NASB). The "vision" Solomon cites is a revelation delivered through a prophet. If the prophet fails to reveal his message, the fate of the people is sealed. Ignorant of the message, the people live a godless life and fall under judgment. The people urgently need the prophet's visionary message.

You have studied these ten Christlike principles for your workplace and you have been given a framework to deploy these God-honoring qualities. Now you have two visions: the vision of new life in Christ and the vision of communicating that new life in your workplace. You have a life-changing message, and you have written down your vision for taking that message to your workplace. Your vision to capture your workplace for Christ is honoring to our God, consistent with Scripture, and within the legal limits of the law. So, are you still wondering if your effort will have impact? Consider Jesus' effort to speak the truth. Read the Gospels. You will find that Christ dealt with people at their work more than at any other place.

Revival at Utica

Charles Finney, an evangelist during the late 1800s, helped his brother-in-law capture his workplace for Christ. One night, after speaking in Utica, New York, Finney was invited to tour the factory where his brother-in-law was manager. The next morning Finney made his way through the production facility. He noticed the workers seemed agitated and excited. Finney spotted one girl who appeared especially nervous. When he got within eight feet of her station, the girl broke down. Emotion swept the factory. The owner of the factory was not a Christian, but he took a stand. He ordered the factory to cease work to "let the people attend to religion; for it is more important that souls should be saved than this factory run."[1]

Who was the workplace prophet in Utica? Was it Finney? Maybe it was Finney's brother-in-law or even the unsaved owner of the factory? I can well imagine that the manager of the factory had been praying for his unbelieving boss. Maybe he had planted the seed for such a workplace gathering over the years and when God's activity collided with the life of the boss, his heart softened to the message of Christ. I believe there were two prophets in Utica. Finney preached the message, and his brother-in-law managed the method of delivery. Only God could have arranged for the opportunity to share His word in the factory owned by one who was lost! Likewise, only God could have brought you to this point in your walk with Him. However unlike Utica, God may have chosen only one prophet for your workplace—you. You have the message and you have the method. You have the vision.

Chapman's Christlike Competitiveness

Dr. Lewis Chapman is an orthodontist with a large practice, a very large practice. Chapman's flourishing practice distorts a key statistic—orthodontists per capita—that new orthodontists study when choosing a city to set up their practices. Dr. Foch Smart graduated as an orthodontist in 1995. He located a city in need of a new practice based on the orthodontists-per-capita ratio.

Smart moved to his new home and began calling on the area dentists. One by one, the dentists suggested Foch visit Dr. Lewis Chapman. Foch now understood why that key ratio looked so favorable: Chapman had a virtual monopoly in the area because the dentists were very loyal to him.

Smart visited Chapman's office. Meeting with your competitor is usually an unpleasant experience, but this meeting was different. Chapman greeted Foch warmly. The two orthodontists talked for more than an hour.

That conversation led Chapman to believe Foch could benefit from his experience. One day after their initial meeting, Chapman sent a few of his employees over to Smart's office. Chapman's people showed Smart how they managed the appointment and bookkeeping processes. Then to Smart's surprise, they called many of the dentists in town and said, "This is Glenda with Dr. Chapman's office. Dr. Chapman wants you to know that Dr. Smart is in town. Dr. Chapman asked me to call you and ask you to refer some patients to Dr. Smart."

Why this uncommon form of competitiveness? Chapman is a Christian who seeks to transform his workplace for Christ. Each morning before his patients arrive, the entire office staff gathers for prayer. His waiting room is full of Christian reading material. Chapman's appointment reminders end with a verse of Scripture. His vision is not limited by the walls of his office. Smart, also a dynamic Christian, was humbled and encouraged by Chapman's actions.

This is an unusual story, but there is more to tell. When Chapman first started his practice some years ago, he was not a Christian. Through the witness of several members of the dental

community, he accepted Christ. Years before, someone sought to capture their workplace for Christ and Lewis Chapman was changed for
eternity. Since then, Chapman has sought opportunities to share
Christ.

A vision for transforming your workplace for Christ impacts
future generations with the eternal message. Ask Dr. Smart. You
have the message, and you have the method. You have the vision.

Your Vision Is Vital

I began to see my coworkers and my workplace differently when I
accepted God's call to be a workplace prophet. Viewing the people
on my job site through the eyes of Christ, I immediately realized the
need to bring my faith to my work.

A Starved Work Force

As you have read this book, you have met people who were
starved for the truth of Christ, but they were either too proud to
admit it or too hardened to accept it. These were real people, many
of whom I encountered at different stops along my career path.
There are people like them in your workplace too.

Finney spoke of the young lady in the factory who appeared
agitated, nervous by his presence. That was an outward sign of an
inner hunger. When Finney approached her, she began to cry. That
may happen today, but it is equally possible that our lost coworkers
will respond to the emptiness in their soul with anger or hostility.
The signs of spiritually starved people are all around us, and we are
God's prophets carrying food for their souls.

A Hostile Environment

You have seen the self-centeredness of our workplace worlds.
Many of us work today to create the cash for self-indulgence, the
wherewithal for self-reliance, and the position for self-image. Our
world emphasizes self, but such self-centeredness is hostile to the
cause of Christ. Consider this observation: "We have grown in numbers, wealth, and power as no other nation has ever grown. But we
have forgotten God. . . . Intoxicated with unbroken success, we have

become too self-sufficient to feel the necessity of redeeming and pre-serving grace, too proud to pray to the God that made us!"[2] Who made this insightful observation about our society? Was it a sociolo-gist or a preacher? A captain of industry? This observation about society was made by Abraham Lincoln in 1863. It appears that Americans have learned very little since then, and today we are reap-ing the results.

It is self-centeredness that causes our insecurities and fear. Many people are scared of litigation. Good activities such as the com-pany picnic have been canceled due to the fear that an injury may result in litigation. Even better activities such as capturing your workplace for Christ don't get off the ground due to the fear of lit-igation. When I began to transform my workplace for Christ, some people, including Christians, thought the idea was wrought with legal problems. I studied it and sought legal advice. You are *not* legally prohibited from transforming your workplace for Christ in the way described in this book. Don't be afraid to seek legal aid.

Time Is of the Essence

On April 3, 1995, an Air Force jet carrying Secretary of Commerce Ron Brown and about thirty-three others, including CEOs from American businesses, crashed in Croatia. The crash occurred in a remote area, and information was very slow to come. In the dark hours that followed the revelation of the accident, the companies of the executives on the trip and Ron Brown's Commerce Department were overcome by the enormity of the news. One employee of an affected company was quoted as saying, "Lord, don't take these people away." Certainly she was expressing her desire for the return of her boss. But maybe she wished for his return because she knew there was some unfinished spiritual business she needed to complete.

One executive canceled his participation in the trip just hours before the departure. When told of the accident, he still had the trip's itinerary in his coat pocket. That executive said, "You think about things left undone and now you're going to get a chance to do them. And you think about things you probably should have done differently."[3]

What an opportunity! Getting things right with God prior to life crashing in. That is an opportunity many people do not have because often those of us who have the answer fail to communicate it. The answer is Jesus Christ, and He has called us to be His workplace prophets before time runs out in this world for our starved and often hostile coworkers. Time is of the essence. Just ask the coworkers of those killed in the Croatian crash!

Your Witness Is Honored

Nothing has been more fulfilling to me in my career than accepting God's call to transform my workplace for Christ. Through God's activity, He allowed me to see a number of people come to know Christ and to see inactive believers reactivate their faith. I have seen what God can do when one person claims His workplace calling and trusts God to work through him.

We go into a hostile environment filled with people who are starved for the gospel, who have a short and unpredictable life span. But we do not go alone. We go with God, the Almighty and the Everlasting. He has given us a vision complete with a life-changing, life-saving message and an effective method of communicating that message. Will you accept His call to ministry? Will you unleash the message of hope in Christ to your coworkers by using your sight to cast a Christlike vision? My prayers are with you. May God bless your ministry!

Notes

Chapter 4
1. Lee Smith, "Stamina: Who Has It, Why You Need It, How to Get It," *Fortune*, 28 November 1994, 127.
2. James C. Dobson, *Hide or Seek*, rev. ed. (Pomona, Calif.: Focus on the Family, 1979), 144–145.

Chapter 5
1. Mark Maremont, "Blind Ambition," *Business Week*, 23 October 1995, 78.
2. Michaels Opinion Research, Inc., "Declining Values: Myth Or Reality?," *The Numbers News*, December 1995, 5.
3. Jeff Down, "Survey: Americans Reluctant to Take Blame for Problems," *The Montgomery Advertiser*, 21 November 1994, 5A.

Chapter 6
1. Cal Ripken, Jr., "Do the Job When It's Not Always Easy," *USA Weekend*, 15 October 1995, taken off Internet.
2. Ibid.
3. Ibid.

Chapter 8
1. S. Truett Cathy, *It Is Easier to Succeed Than Fail* (Nashville: Thomas Nelson, 1989), 69–70.

2. Ibid.
3. Ibid., 76–77.
4. Ibid., 75.

Chapter 10
1. This is an awesome Christ-centered camp. For more information, write to Kanakuk-Kanakomo Kamp, 1353 Lakeshore Drive, Branson, Missouri 65616.

Chapter 12
1. Mark D. Roberts, *The Communicators Commentary, Ezra, Nehemiah, Esther* (Waco, Texas: Word, 1993), 176.

Chapter 14
1. John Kramp, *Out of Their Faces and into Their Shoes* (Nashville: Broadman and Holman, 1995).
2. John Trent and Rick Hicks, *Seeking Solid Ground* (Colorado Springs: Focus on the Family, 1995).
3. Gene Getz, *David: Seeking God Faithfully* (Men of Character series) (Nashville: Broadman and Holman, 1995).
4. Charles R. Swindoll, *The Grace Awakening* (Dallas: Word, 1990).
5. John Trent, *LifeMapping* (Colorado Springs: Focus on the Family, 1994).
6. Ravi Zacharias, *Can Man Live without God?* (Dallas: Word, 1994).
7. Robert J. Tamasy, *Jesus Works Here* (Nashville: Broadman and Holman, 1995).

Conclusion
1. Charles G. Finney, *Memoirs* (New York: Fleming Revell, 1876), 183–184.
2. *USA Today*, 23 November 1994, 5A.
3. *USA Today*, 4 April, 1995, 2B.